W0027845

ISANDLWANA 1879

ISANDLWANA 1879

EDMUND YORKE

For Louise, Madeleine and Emily

First published 2011
This edition published 2015

Spellmount, an imprint of
The History Press
The Mill, Brimscombe Port
Stroud, Gloucestershire, GL5 2QG
www.thehistorypress.co.uk

© The History Press, 2011, 2015

The right of Edmund Yorke to be identified as the Author of this work has been asserted in accordance with the Copyrights, Designs and Patents Act 1988.

All rights reserved. No part of this book may be reprinted or reproduced or utilised in any form or by any electronic, mechanical or other means, now known or hereafter invented, including photocopying and recording, or in any information storage or retrieval system, without the permission in writing from the Publishers.

British Library Cataloguing in Publication Data.
A catalogue record for this book is available from the British Library.

ISBN 978 0 7509 6523 1

Typesetting and origination by The History Press
Printed in India

CONTENTS

ACKNOWLEDGEMENTS

I wish to express my gratitude to many individuals who contributed to this work. The librarians, curators and archivists of the Universities of Oxford and Cambridge, the National Army Museum, the London Library, the Public Record Office at Kew, and the South Wales Borderers Museum in Brecon have been particularly helpful. Andrew Orgill, Senior Librarian of RMA Sandhurst Library, and his assistants, Ken Franklin and John Pearce, have provided their usual sterling and exceptional support. The Commissioning Editor Jo de Vries and her team at the History Press have also provided invaluable advice and encouragement.

The works and advice of several authors and experts in the field, notably Professor John Laband, Mr Ian Knight, Mr F.W. Jackson, John Young, Ron Lock, Peter Quantrill, Lieutenant Colonel Mike Snook and the late, much lamented David Rattray, Donald Morris and Frank Emery, have, over the years, jointly provided great inspiration for this book. My most recent 2004 visit to the Isandlwana battlefield and attendance at the splendid 125th commemorative dinner held in Isandlwana Lodge, so charmingly hosted by Pat Stubbs, enabled me to renew many old acquaintances and to make many new ones. Major Andrew Banks and John Young both provided excellent pictorial support from their extensive private collections to supplement my own field photographs. F.W. Jackson has been a source of great advice and encouragement, and the several meetings and dinners we have recently enjoyed together remain treasured memories. Mrs Susan Coleridge, currently working on a major reappraisal of the life of Colonel Anthony Durnford, has been a most useful source of information, especially on Durnford's still controversial role at Isandlwana. Above all, I must thank my great friend Colonel Ian Bennett (RLC retired). Our regular triennial lunches at Sandhurst and joint excursions and research trips have been a wonderful source of intellectual advice and encouragement. Several of my colleagues at RMA Sandhurst have also been of great help, notably my current Head of Department, Dr Duncan Anderson MA, Dr Gregory Fremont-Barnes, Professor Christopher Duffy, Dr Matthew Bennett and Mr Sean McKnight, MA, Director of Studies. Mention must also be made of the scores of officer-cadets and commissioned officers who, over the past twenty-two years, have shared my great enthusiasm for this famous battle.

Above all I must express my deep love and appreciation for the long-suffering support of my dear wife Louise and daughters, Madeleine and Emily, the former for the long tedious hours of rapid word processing of reams of documents and indecipherable notes, and, the latter, for the many hours of neglect by their elusive Daddy. I also wish to thank my dear family, especially my parents and elder sister, Liz, (the latter braved the many 2004 Isandlwana battlefield treks and mad obsessions of her brother), who have been an enormous source of encouragement and enthusiasm.

LIST OF ILLUSTRATIONS

11 A typical Zulu warrior. Zulu boys would be taught basic economic and military skills at military kraals, known as '*amakhanda*'. (AB)

12 A classic, accurate engraving of a Zulu charge. Note the deployment of muskets alongside traditional spears and assegais. (EY)

13 Zulu warrior group (AB)

14 Colonel R.T. Glyn, Commander of No. 3 Column and heavily criticised in Chelmsford's recently discovered memo of February 1879. (RRWM)

15 The swotting of a 'Zulu wasp' by the British lion. This 1879 *Punch* cartoon graphically shows that the Zulu threat was only one of several problems besetting the hard-pressed Disraeli government.

16 The perils of campaigning in Zululand, *Punch*, August 1879.

17 A rare contemporary view of Rorke's Drift crossing point on the Mzinyathi (Buffalo) River. (JY)

18 Commissariat stores on the Lower Tulega. (JY)

19 Lord Chelmsford, pictured after the Zulu War. (JY)

20 A watercolour copy of Colonel Crealock's evocative 20/21 January paintings of the Isandlwana Camp. A deceptively tranquil scene with a lone sentry and cattle lazily grazing. A few hours later it was to be the scene of a terrible massacre. (EY)

21 Lieutenant Charles D'Aguilar Pope. (RRWM)

22 Map of the Isandlwana battle around 1pm.

23 A rough sketch of the Isandlwana campsite. (C.L. Norris-Newman, *In Zululand with the British* (Allen & Co., 1880))

24 Captain Reginald Younghusband, 24th Regiment. (JY)

25 An extremely rare photograph of Captain George Wardell's 1/24th H Company, annihilated at Isandlwana. (RRWM)

26 Lieutenant Mainwaring's sketch and watercolour of the Isandlwana Campaign. (RRWM)

27 Brevet Colonel Anthony William Durnford (1830–79) whose aggressive tactics at Isandlwana may have fatally compromised Pulleine. (JY)

45–50 Officers who fell at Isandlwana (clockwise from top left): 45 Henry Julien Dyer. 46 James Patrick Daly. 47 George Frederick John Hodson. 48 Frederick Godwin-Austen. 49 William Degacher. 50 Thomas Llewelyn George Griffith. (RRWM)

51 Fugitive's Drift 1989: the cross marks the spot where Melvill and Coghill were found. (EY)

52 The Queen's Colour (on the left) is the colour rescued from Buffalo River after Isandlwana. (RRWM)

53 The rocky terrain and rough scrub which must have impeded the final British retreat to the tented area below the mountain. (EY)

54 Edward Bloomfield 2/24th, one of two quartermasters who controlled the logistical lifelines at Isandlwana. (RRWM)

55 Quartermaster James Pullen 1/24th. (RRWM)

56 Lieutenant Horace Smith-Dorrien as a brigadier general. (JY)

57 Francis Pender Porteous, imperial officer of the 24th Regiment. (RRWM)

58 An unusual view of Isandlwana from Fugitive's Drift, where the Undi Corps begain its advance on Rorke's Drift. (EY)

59 Lieutenant General Sir Garnet Wolseley, who superceded Chelmsford as commander-in-chief, but became embittered when Chelmsford thwarted his opportunity for glory by finally breaking Zulu power at Ulundi. (JY)

60 A satirical comment on Wolseley's final capture of the elusive Cetshwayo long after the British victory at Ulundi, from *Punch*, September 1879. (EY)

61 In this *Punch* cartoon Lieutenants Chard and Bromhead are saluted for their gallant defence at Rorke's Drift, March 1879.

Front cover: A detail from a painting of British troops fighting against Zulu warriors from the Undi Corps. (Richard Scollins)

INTRODUCTION

I regret to have to report a very disastrous engagement which took place on the 22nd January, between the Zulus and a portion of No. 3 Column ... the Zulus came down in overwhelming numbers and but a few of its defenders escaped.

Chelmsford to Secretary of State Colonies, 10 February 1879, Vic/O/33, Royal Archives, Windsor

We returned to Isandlwana. We arrived early in the morning – we went to see the dead people we saw a single warrior dead, staring in our direction, with his war shield in his hand ... we saw countless things dead. Dead was the horse, dead too, the mule, dead was the dog... dead were the wagons, dead were the tents, dead were the boxes, dead was everything, even to the very metals... We saw white men dead (they had taken off their boots, all of them) and the people also who had served with them and fought with them, and some Zulus, but not many...'

'A Zulu Boy's Recollection of the Zulu War', *Natalia*, December 1978

A remarkable people the Zulu. They defeat our generals; convert our Bishops and put an end to a great European dynasty.

Benjamin Disraeli, 1879

The battle of Isandlwana remains one of the most iconic battles in British imperial and military history. In probably little more than two hours of fighting, a garrison comprising around 1,700 British regular, colonial and African auxiliary forces were overwhelmed and practically annihilated by an estimated 20–25,000-strong Zulu Army. Over 1,300 men on the British side perished in this pitiless, savage and often hand-to-hand encounter, their bodies remaining unburied for several months after the battle. It has been claimed that more British regular and colonial officers were killed at Isandlwana than at the Battle of Waterloo. For the Zulu nation the battle was equally iconic. It represented the high tide of Zulu nationalism and a rare, indeed stunning victory in the broader nineteenth-century struggle of indigenous peoples against rampant colonialism. Only a few other global examples of indigenous victories, notably the destruction of Major General Elphinstone's 16,000-strong Anglo-Indian army by an estimated 10,000 Afghan irregulars in 1842, the complete annihilation of General Custer's 200-strong 7th cavalry force by 8,000 Sioux/Cheyenne in 1876 and the rout of an Italian army at Adowa by Ethiopian warriors in 1896, bear comparison in terms of both the scale of defeat and the impact that they had on their respective colonial establishments.

The main aim of this short introductory book is to, by using revised material drawn mainly from my extensive published literature on the Anglo-Zulu War, my own fieldwork studies of the Isandlwana battlefield in 1989 and 2004, as well as that of several selected leading contemporary experts, present for non-specialists and general history enthusiasts, a clear, hopefully balanced and concise analytical narrative of this epic encounter. The opinions expressed in this book are my own and do not reflect those of either the Ministry of Defence or the Royal Military Academy Sandhurst.

TIMELINE

1652–1872

1652	Dutch occupy Cape of South Africa
1806	Britain occupies Cape
1814	Britain annexes the Cape
1816	Zulu Chief Shaka ascends Zulu throne
1816–1828	Paramount Chief Shaka expands and consolidates the Zulu Empire
1828	Shaka is assassinated
1830s	Boer communities commence Great Treks away from British rule into the Southern African interior and clash with Zulu clans, culminating in the Piet Retief massacre
1838	Boer commandoes defeat main Zulu Army at Blood River (Ncome)
1843	Natal officially declared a British colony
1850s	Foundation of the Independent Boer Republics of the Orange Free State and the Transvaal. Diamond discoveries in the Orange Free State

1873–1878

1873	King Cetshwayo Ka Mpande crowned king of the Zulu nation
1875	Lord Carnarvon officially launches South African Confederation policy
April 1877	Transvaal annexed by Britain. Sir H.B. Frere appointed Governor and High Commissioner for South Africa to execute Confederation policy
1878	Murder of Zulu women on Natal side of the border
11 December 1878	British ultimatum delivered to Cetshwayo's Zulu emissaries at the Lower Thukela Drift

1879

11 January	British ultimatum expires and British troops enter Zululand under the overall command of Lord Chelmsford
12 January	British No. 3 Centre Column successfully attacks Sihayo's kraal (settlement) in the Batshe Valley
17 January	Main Zulu Army leaves Ulundi or oNdini
18 January	Section of main Zulu Army leaves to challenge British column in coastal sector. Majority of main Zulu Army approaches British No. 3 Centre Column
20 January	British Centre Column advances and establish camp beneath Isandlwana Crag. Lord Chelmsford and his staff reconnoitre Hlazakazi range. Colonel Durnford's No. 2 Column establishes camp at Rorke's Drift
21 January	Mounted contingents and Natal Native Contingent (NNC) under overall command of Major Dartnell reconnoitre Malakathi and Hlazakazi hills. Clashes with Zulu units near Mangeni in late afternoon. Main Zulu Army covertly moves from Siphezi hill and bivouacks in Ngwebeni Valley

1879

22 January	Chelmsford departs camp, with half the British garrison. Zulu victory at Battle of Isandlwana. British victories at the battles of Rorke's Drift and Nyezane
February/ March	British reinforcements pour into South Africa
29 March	Decisive British victory at the Battle of Khambula
2 April	British victory at Battle of Gingindlovu
4 July	British achieve final victory at Battle of Ulundi (oNdini). Zulu royal power effectively broken. Anglo-Zulu War ends

HISTORICAL BACKGROUND

The origins of the 1879 Anglo-Zulu War, which commenced so disastrously with the catastrophic British defeat at Isandlwana, can be traced back many years. Its roots can be seen in the violent and turbulent relationships existing between European settler societies and indigenous African peoples, which had reached crisis point by the late nineteenth century. South Africa, fast emerging as one of Britain's wealthiest if most complex and difficult colonies, was facing political meltdown. By January 1878, Lord Carnarvon's grand confederation scheme, designed to create a modern, unified, self-governing and, above all, a loyal and economical dominion of the British Empire, was on the verge of disintegration. Strenuous efforts over the previous decade to achieve political and economic unity had made little progress. While three out of the five white-settler states, the Cape, Natal and Griqualand West, were under British rule by 1876, no two communities could agree on a common future. Old inter-colonial, often commercial, jealousies, such as those existing between the Cape and Natal, remained potent obstacles to imperial confederation. The other two white-settler colonies, the Orange Free State and the Transvaal, remained extremely hostile to the idea of British rule. It was a long and deep hostility dating back to the 'Great Trek' of the

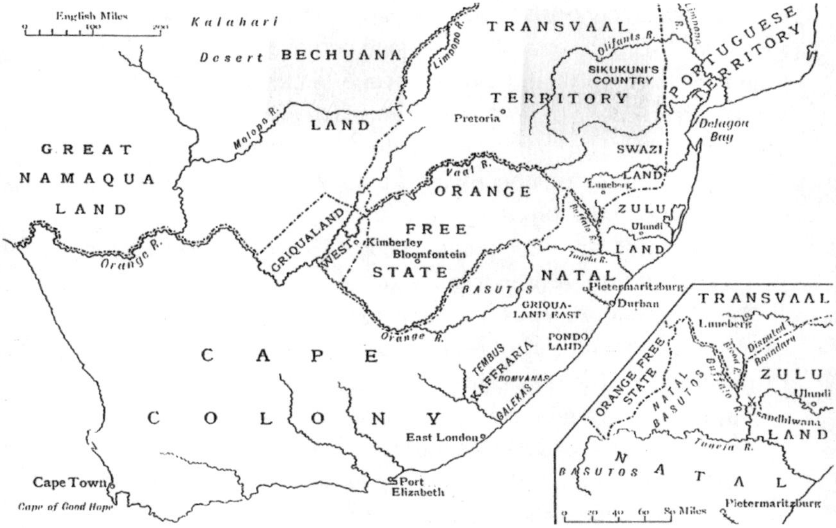

1. Sketch map of South Africa, 1879.

Lord Carnarvon and the Grand Confederation Scheme

Lord Carnarvon, as the British Secretary of State for the Colonies during the 1870s, believed strongly in the idea of confederation, i.e. the uniting of separate 'states' into a self-governing whole under the ultimate power of the British Empire. This would, in practice, mean that the settlers would be able to legislate on their own behalf and make decisions directly relevant to the colony, as long as they were in line with imperial policy. It has been suggested that one of Carnarvon's motivations for confederation in South Africa was also to protect the black population from the white settlers, however the South African Act of 1877 actually restricted the native population from having any voice in the federal assembly.

1830s when hundreds of Boer families, mostly descendants of the original Dutch colonisers of the Cape before British annexation, had trekked north and east to escape the pressures of British authority, especially new tax and anti-slavery laws. The wealthier Orange Free State remained solidly independent from British rule and was already benefiting from the earlier diamond field discoveries of the 1860s. By stark contrast, the under-populated Transvaal was facing bankruptcy and imminent collapse under the pressure of local African tribes and was in danger of creating a serious security vacuum for the imperial authorities.

The state of African affairs was equally worrying for the British government. The Cape-Xhosa War was in full swing and other outbreaks were predicted. The earlier diamond discoveries in Griqualand West and the Orange Free State during the 1860s and 1870s, and the consequent accelerated demand for black labour had hastened the break-up of tribal societies and greatly magnified overall regional tension. As Lord Carnarvon remarked in a letter to British High Commissioner Sir Bartle Frere, there were 'clouds gathering all around the horizon' and no cloud was perceived to be more ominous and threatening than the Zulu 'thundercloud' overshadowing the isolated and highly vulnerable British colony of Natal and the crumbling Transvaal state.

Friction and war between these groups of European settlers and the Zulu, the most powerful African tribe in sub-Saharan Africa, had

Cape-Xhosa War

Alternatively referred to as the Xhosa Wars, Cape Frontier Wars or Kaffir Wars, these were a series of nine conflicts between the native Xhosa tribe and white European (often Boer) settlers in the Eastern Cape of South Africa. They raged from 1779 to 1879 and resulted in the Xhosa people losing most of their land. The ninth, and final, war saw the Xhosa territory being incorporated into the Cape Colony.

been a recurring feature of the previous half-century. Major conflict between the Boers and the Zulu dated from at least the 1830s when migrating trekkers had first clashed with Zulu *impis* (regiments) as they pushed deep into the southern African interior. The great Zulu Empire, forged, as we shall see, by war, from a few disparate Nguni clans led by Chief Shaka, had, by the 1870s, come to dominate much of the south-east region of South Africa, and deployed an estimated 40,000 warriors. Nevertheless, until then the tiny British colony of Natal (established in 1845), despite its precarious position alongside the Zulu kingdom, had maintained relatively amicable relations with successive Zulu chieftains and British imperial forces, and had not been drawn into any full-scale conflict with them. Indeed, the British settlers of Natal were already seen as natural rivals or even enemies by many Boers who feared renewed British encirclement and consequently were willingly courted as friends, if not allies, by the Zulus who understandably preferred them to their more hostile and aggressive Boer neighbours. As even the British High Commissioner Frere later admitted, the Zulu under their chief, Cetshwayo, were:

> always anti-Boer and therefore philo-Natal, and one sees a good deal of the feeling for him thus engendered among people here, some of whom would sooner see us join the Zulus to teach the Boers manners, than join the Boers to prevent the Zulus from murdering.
>
> Martineau, *Life*, 2, Frere to Herbert, 23 December 1878

In April 1877, however, a single legal act transformed Anglo-Zulu relations for the worse and, from the strategic and security perspective of several senior and local imperial officials, inexorably propelled the British and Zulu nations along the road to war. The British annexation of the bankrupt Transvaal by the British Administrator, Sir Theophilus Shepstone, an act sanctioned and carried out on behalf of Lord Carnarvon, has been recognised by most historians as a primary catalyst of the Zulu War. B.C. Pine, a former Natal governor, described it in the *Contemporary Review* (June 1879) as the 'immediate cause of the Zulu War', with the annexation effectively destroying the 'system of checks and balances' whereby Natal had been safeguarded from Zulu attack by the existence of an independent Transvaal as a counterpoise or buffer. In Shepstone's words:

> Hitherto the relations of the Amaswazi Zulu with Her Majesty's Government has been from circumstances of distant neighbours but by, that recent change, they had become either adjoining neighbours or subjects.
>
> CO, 48/482, Shepstone to Carnarvon, 27 May 1877

Sir Bartle Frere, the newly arrived High Commissioner, painted a more allegorical picture of this nonetheless serious security dilemma for British authority created by the event:

> The fact is that while the Boer Republic was a rival and semi-hostile power, it was a Natal weakness rather to pet the Zulus as one might a tame wolf who only devours ones neighbours sheep. We always remonstrated, but rather feebly, and now that both flocks belong to us we are rather embarrassed in stopping the wolf's ravages.
>
> RA, Queen Victoria's Journal, Frere to Ponsonby

The Zulu 'wolf' was now at Natal's door, precipitating a tense face-to-face confrontation between British power and Zulu power along a far wider strategic front. According to at least one expert and contemporary observer, the acclaimed author and Africanist Sir Henry Rider Haggard, this dramatic strategic change made Zulu Chief Cetshwayo deeply suspicious and hostile to what appeared to him to be a concerted attempt at the encirclement of his Zulu kingdom by his former British friends.

Individual responsibility for embarking on the disastrous road to war remains an area of great controversy among historians.

2. The Earl of Carnarvon, the primary catalyst behind the South African Confederation. (JY)

Of the five key colonial officials most directly involved in this 'war policy' against the Zulu nation – notably Sir Theophilus Shepstone, Administrator of the Transvaal, Lieutenant General Frederick Thesiger (later Lord Chelmsford), Commander-in-Chief, British forces South Africa, and Sir Michael Hicks Beach, Colonial Secretary – it has been the British High Commissioner for South Africa, Sir Henry Bartle Edward Frere who has been largely blamed for this ultimately tragic and bloody confrontation. Thus leading historians have variously described Frere as an aggressive, unprincipled expansionist, 'a man of tenacious character and grave and lofty, if ill-calculated aims' and a man who, 'by his high-handed conduct plunged the country into an idle and indefensible war against the Zulu'. Others, including myself, whilst not denying that Frere fully shared the imperial attitudes and prejudices of his generation, perceive him to be a man confronted by a virtually impossible security dilemma that was greatly magnified by the ambivalent behaviour of leading colonial officials both at home and on the spot in South Africa.

Frere had in fact freshly arrived from India with an awesome reputation both as a leading imperial statesman and as a highly skilled troubleshooter. Renowned South African historian C.W. De Kiewiet observed that 'no South African Governor had come so rich in varied experience'. A man perceived by many to be of the highest honour and integrity, he had, for nine years, been Chief Commissioner of Sind, where his courageous record during the Indian Mutiny had moved none other than Sir John Lawrence (Viceroy of India) to observe that, 'probably there is no Civil Officer, who, for eminent exertion, deserves better of this Government than

3. Sir Henry Bartle Edward Frere (1815–84), Governor of the Cape and High Commissioner for South Africa since 1877, entrusted with the arduous task of completing Lord Carnarvon's ailing confederation scheme. (JY)

Mr H.E.B. Frere'. Why, after his elevated career in India, Frere should be interested in this less prestigious post is a mystery but the historian Saul David is probably right in suggesting that Frere was lured both by the prospects of a peerage and the complex challenge of confederation which, if successful, would make him South Africa's first governor general with a salary rising from £7,000 to £10,000 after successful confederation: 'It was all too much for a man of Frere's vanity, ambition and impecunity to resist'.

By stark contrast to this renowned colonial veteran, Frere's new political master, Colonial Secretary Sir Michael Hicks Beach, possessed virtually no experience in colonial administration. Even his arch-defender and biographer, Lady Hicks Beach, conceded that he became colonial secretary 'with no special knowledge of South African affairs'. It boded ill for a minister in charge of one of Britain's most difficult and complicated colonies. He was a loyal Disraelite and, as historian C.F. Goodfellow observed 'it was probably his loyalty, as much as his ability which had produced his elevation to the Cabinet while still Chief Secretary for Ireland in November 1876'.

His great inexperience clearly showed in his early correspondence with Frere. During the first exchange of letters between the two men, an ill-at-ease Hicks Beach readily confessed that he was a 'poor substitute for Carnarvon' and, rather reminiscent of a pupil addressing his schoolmaster, informed Frere that, 'I have been doing my best to make myself acquainted with my new work and more especially with South African Affairs'.

Frere was immediately given wide discretion to complete Carnarvon's confederation policies. In one letter, Sir Michael thus assured Frere of his 'anxiety to co-operate with you in every possible way', and that he hardly feels in a position to express any opinions on South African affairs. Frere was encouraged to take his own initiative and promised 'support and co-operation in your difficult position which you have a right to expect from anyone here'. Twelve months later, Frere might well have wondered why such support was not forthcoming.

Frere was now plunged into a virtual political vacuum as he proceeded to grapple with the twin problems of implementing the confederation and addressing the new security issues of Natal and Transvaal. A number of incidents on the British Transvaal and Natal borders hastened the two empires along the road to war over the next twenty months. At the centre of the tension was the long-standing and urgent problem of the boundary dispute between the Zulus and the Transvaal Boers, a problem now reluctantly inherited by Britain. The dispute stemmed from a Boer claim to a strip of land located in the south-east corner of the Transvaal, territory also claimed by Cetshwayo, paramount Zulu Chief since 1873. With annexation, this was now a major British problem, and in February 1878, in response to frequent Zulu protest, the Natal Governor, Sir Henry Bulwer, established a commission to arbitrate the dispute.

By that time, Sir Bartle Frere had decided that, in the strategic interest of achieving a modern 'civilised' confederation, prolonged physical security and with it, hopefully the loyalty of both British and white Boer interests in South Africa, the Zulu Empire would have to be dismantled. In this decision, he had been deeply influenced by Sir Theophilus Shepstone, the new Administrator of the Transvaal, who had initially been an erstwhile friend of Cetshwayo, having attended his coronation in 1873. In October 1877, however, after meeting with Cetshwayo's envoys on the frontier to seek a final settlement to the boundary dispute, he had been met by them in an allegedly 'self asserting, aggressive and defiant spirit'. Thereafter, Shepstone took an increasingly anti-Zulu and pro-Boer stance in his communications with Frere. By December 1877 he was openly accusing Cetshwayo of violating his coronation promises of 'good government' and the Zulu of acting as a catalyst to all African unrest:

> one thing is certain that if we are forced into hostilities we cannot stop short of breaking down the Zulu power, which after all is the root and the real strength of all native difficulties in South Africa.
> Martineau, *Life*, 2, p.233, Shepstone to Frere, 1 December 1877

With reference to the boundary dispute, he expressed his belief that this 'difficulty is a pre-concerted matter and that Cetshwayo really believes in his power to overcome us all without much difficulty'. By June 1878 such reports had convinced Frere that the Galeka and Gaika risings (the ongoing war with the local Chief Sekhukhune), were the result of a general conspiracy headed by the Zulu 'incubus'. In a crucial despatch to R.W. Herbert, Under Secretary at the Colonial Office, sent in mid-March 1878, Frere expounded these deeply held beliefs:

> I do not think I ever expressed to you my conviction which has been gradually and unwillingly growing, that Shepstone and others of experience in the country, were right as to the existence of a wish among the great Chiefs to make this war a general and simultaneous rising of Kaffirdom against white civilisation.

He continued:

> this conviction has been forced on me by a hundred little bits of evidence from different quarters… and… there was a wide-spread feeling among them [the chiefs], from Secocoeni to Sandilli, that the time has come for them all to join to resist the flood

> of new ideas and ways which threaten to sweep away the idle, sensuous, Elysium of Kaffirdom such as Gaika and Chaka and Dingaan fought for and enjoyed...
>
> Martineau, *Life*, 2, Frere to Herbert, 18 March, 1878

More sinister ulterior motives lay beyond this security problem presented by the Zulu. Cetshwayo's warrior army of up to 40,000 males represented a 'virgin', i.e. untapped, labour pool, presenting a golden opportunity to 'modernise' the Zulu. A break-up of the Zulu Empire would clearly serve the rapacious needs of the mines and farms of white settlerdom. In Shepstone's words:

> had Cetshwayo's 30,000 warriors been in time changed to labourers working for wages, Zululand would now have been a prosperous peaceful country instead of what it now is, a source of perpetual danger to itself and its neighbours.
>
> RA, Queen Victoria's Journal (1878)

But for Sir Bartle Frere, it was above all a security problem. He knew from his bitter experiences, particularly during the Indian Mutiny but also in the Sind, the Punjab and Afghanistan, where 'native conspiracies' were seen to be rife, that a robust forward policy was essential – there could be no uncertainty as to whether European or 'native' power was the strongest. In his concept of a strong 'Pax Britannica', a civilised and uncivilised power could not exist peaceably side by side as European nations could, unless the uncivilised power distinctly recognised that it was the weaker of the two and that it must in essentials conform to the civic standard of right and wrong of the other. Thus in an 1863 Minute, Frere defined the English 'frontier system' as 'a reserve of physical force amply sufficient to enforce its moral obligations whenever an appeal to physical force was inevitable'. This was not as arbitrary and ruthless as it seemed, as he also stressed that force should only be employed when conciliatory methods such as attempts at open diplomacy and good neighbourliness had been exhausted.

Sekhukhune/Pedi Wars

Sekhukhune was the formidable chief of the Pedi tribe, who were based at the time in the Transvaal. The Pedi lived in a state of constant friction with their Boer neighbours over land rights and disputes over cattle (which the Boer claimed the Pedi were stealing from them). This conflict finally descended into war, with fighting in 1876 and then erupting again in 1878–79. In 1879 the wars came to an effective end when the imperial-led Transvaal Field Force captured Sekhukhune.

For Frere and other leading officials, the events of the past two years (1876–78), including the period before Frere had arrived, had already undermined any concept of 'good neighbourliness' with the Zulu. In late 1876, an official protest sent to the Zulu King Cetshwayo by the normally 'Zulu-phile' Natal Governor, Sir Henry Bulwer, concerning the slaughter of a number of Zulu maidens as punishment for marrying into traditionally celibate Zulu regiments, had led to an aggressive warning from Cetshwayo against interference in Zulu internal affairs.

Consequently, Bulwer sent a strongly worded despatch to Carnarvon, in which he described Cetshwayo as expressing 'a great desire for war' and that information had reached him that Cetshwayo 'had not only been preparing for war but that he had been sounding the way with a view to a combination of the native races against the white men'. The fact that these words were written by one of the formerly staunchest of pro-Zulu politicians in Natal is indicative of the deterioration that was occurring in Anglo-Zulu relations. Missionary reports of the persecution, even murder, of their Zulu converts further convinced Frere of the need for decisive action; evidence of gun running to the Zulu by unscrupulous (mainly Portuguese) traders in the Delagoa Bay region, and of the apparent increased German infiltration into the region, also increased Frere's security fears.

By the spring of 1878, this evidence confirmed to Frere that the success of his 'Grand Design', the final push to confederation, rested on the elimination of the Zulu menace. If Frere's policy was, in Goodfellow's words:

> no more than Carnarvon's policy pricked from a canter to a gallop by the presence in South Africa of a man who combined the authority to initiate with a capacity to execute...
>
> C.F. Goodfellow, *Great Britain and South African Confederation*, pp.166–67

It did, nevertheless, reflect a new sense of dynamism and spirit of optimism. In the spring and summer of 1878, these forward policy moves received the wide and unqualified support of both the inexperienced Hicks Beach and his senior, more experienced, Colonial Office officials. In March 1878, Hicks Beach gave Frere even greater support and powers of discretion, agreeing:

> that the presence of a considerable force in Natal with some... augmentation of that in the Transvaal could not be without its useful effect on Cetshwayo.
>
> St Aldwyn/Hicks Beach Papers, Hicks Beach to Frere, 7 March 1878

As Bulwer negotiated the boundary dispute between the Zulu and Transvaal Boers, Hicks Beach agreed that they should be 'pushed on', and that the 'dwellers in the disputed territory be protected from aggression...' One month later, Hicks Beach actively supported a military build up: 'the movement of troops to the Transvaal and Natal especially the former, seems very desirable in order to impress both the Boers and the Zulus.'

By June 1878, Frere was entrusted with even greater initiative by Hicks Beach and told that not only should he personally supervise the boundary dispute, but 'when you do arbitrate, your arbitration must be upheld at whatever cost'. The Boundary Commission's findings published in June 1878 and ruling in favour of the Zulus, were an unwelcome surprise, but did not deflect Frere from his broader

4. Sir Michael Hicks Beach, Secretary of State for the Colonies. (JY)

concept of breaking up Zulu power, and he effectively reserved decision on the matter. Home government support continued for both his formal Zulu policy and a wider extension of British control under Carnarvon's confederation concept. When, for instance, he extended imperial control over Pondoland and the St John's River, he received constant encouragement and even praise for his bold initiatives. On the annexation of Pondoland, for instance, one senior Colonial Office official, Pearson, wrote:

> I think Sir Bartle Frere was right in acting upon his own judgement without waiting for authority from home as a weak Governor might have done… the occasion came at a critical time when hesitation or delay might have been attended with serious results.
>
> CO 48/486, Pearson Minute, 24 September 1878

Such words of encouragement must have again resonated in Frere's ears as he faced censure for his Zulu War policies a mere six months later. Another Colonial Office official, Edward Wingfield, similarly expressed the hope that:

> Natal will be sensible of the importance of securing a position of commanding influence over Pondoland in the event of war with the Zulus and will appreciate the steps taken by Sir Bartle Frere for that purpose.
>
> CO 48/485, Wingfield Comment

The July 1878 kidnapping and brutal murder (by garrotting) of two allegedly adulterous Zulu women who had fled across the border, carried out by the sons (principally Mehlokazulu) of Sihayo kaXongo Ngobese, a significant Zulu chieftain, further convinced Frere and leading settlers that the Zulu problem and their 'war fever' must be 'at once grappled with'. In the view of leading historian Ian Knight, this incident was a significant catalyst to war:

> Mehlokazulu's actions highlighted the uncomfortable but increasingly obvious fact that the British and Zulu could not readily accommodate each other – and that two very different cultures, fundamentally opposed to one another, were now in competition for the right to rule.
>
> I. Knight, *Zulu Rising: The Epic Story of Isandlwana and Rorke's Drift*, p.11

In September, while 'on the spot' in Natal, Frere dramatically reported that the people of Natal were now:

> slumbering on a volcano and I much fear that you will not be able to send out the reinforcements we have asked for in time to prevent an explosion... the Zulus are now quite out of hand.
>
> B. Worsfold, p.91, Frere to Hicks Beach, 30 September 1878

A war with the Zulus was imminent. In mid-September Edward Wingfield, a Colonial Office official, scribbled on one of Frere's despatches, 'it seems only too probable... that a Zulu war is imminent'. His senior, Under-Secretary Herbert, went even further:

> It seems certain that there is to be a Zulu war and I see little to hope for except that the resistance of the natives may be weak and the operation soon over.
>
> CO 48/486, Herbert Note, 16 September 1878

Frere accordingly continued with his war preparations assisted by his Commander-in-Chief South Africa, General Lord Chelmsford.

THE ARMIES

The British Forces

The preparations for invading Zululand had taken months. In 1879, the British Army remained a largely cumbersome, hierarchical machine, but one which was well used to victory over 'native enemies' in Africa and elsewhere. The army's extended imperial role as guardians of huge tracts of territory, particularly in Africa and India, had deeply moulded its character and its organisation which differed greatly from other contemporary armies on the continent. Rather than constituting an army in the context of a large field force organised into divisions and corps under a systematic chain of command, it was distinguished by small 'penny packet' formations, often only of battalion size and scattered throughout the empire. Highly mobilised and specialised in order to deal with a wide variety of small colonial wars, it relied heavily on overwhelming superiority of equipment, expecting only minute casualties and easy victories. The British Army was so imperially orientated (with up to fifty battalions based in India after the mutiny of 1857) that it played little part in influencing events in Europe. In 1846, for instance, barely 10,000 men could be found at home to meet a French threat perceived to be imminent. Improvisation was the order of the day, and without the collective high-level command structure of, for instance, the French and German armies, military success often depended on the perceptiveness and resourcefulness of selected commanders such as Lord Roberts, Lord Napier and General Wolseley. Their exploits in, for instance, the Afghan (1878–80) and Ashanti (1874–75) campaigns achieved legendary status in Victorian England, but concealed the inappropriateness of their methodology for any concept of a modern continental-style war. Until the late 1890s, army manoeuvres were still recreating the traditional square formations as practised at the Battle of Waterloo in 1815! The limited role and size of the army also réflected its low priority in terms of government expenditure, and it was not an institution which enjoyed high social esteem during the late eighteenth and early nineteenth centuries. The army's anarchic role in the containment of the 1780 anti-Catholic Gordon Riots, for example, prompted the often-quoted remark by the Whig politician Charles James Fox, that he would 'much rather be governed by a mob than a standing army'. Despite great victories such as at Waterloo, the reputation of the British military at home was further tarnished by the heavy-handed policing actions conducted by both local militia and regular forces during the post-Napoleonic war disturbances and the Chartist disorders of the 1840s. Of these, the 1819 Peterloo Massacre, when a dozen men and women were cut down by the sabres of an ill-disciplined local militia and contingents of regular Hussars, left a legacy of hatred in working-class areas of Lancashire which lingered on for decades.

The army's relatively poor image reflected, to a large extent, the appalling conditions of service and consequent problems of recruitment. Most rank-and-file soldiers were recruited from the lowest levels of Victorian urban and rural society, and were often petty criminals or destitute farm labourers. Before 1870, many recruits had been drawn from Ireland – particularly after the 1840s potato famines – but the great trade depression of the 1870s brought a new influx of urban and rural poor from mainland Britain. By the mid-nineteenth century, service conditions could be brutal, dull and uncompromising and men were expected to sign

5. Officers, NCOs and men of the (1st Battalion, probably) 24th Regiment, pictured in Zululand in 1879. Note the officer's sphinx cap badge, young drummer boy/ musician and the prevalence of beards worn by many of the lower ranks. (RMAS)

on for exceptionally long periods. Up to 1847, men enlisted for life and after that date, for ten years with the option of continuing for twenty-one years to qualify for a pension. Private living space in barracks was often less than that afforded to prison convicts, and mortality rates were often double those of civilians. On meagre unvarying rations of bread, bully beef and biscuits, the Victorian soldier eked out an extremely hard existence. Military life consisted of parades and fatigues with training hardly going beyond eternal drill and sporadic gymnastic exercises. In the late Victorian period, out of a gross pay of around seven shillings a week, half would be deducted for food over and above basic rations, and over a tenth of a soldier's pay was taken for laundry services etc. Week-long field training exercises were confined to six or seven occasions a year, and recreational activity devolved upon regimental canteens and local brothels. In India, the regimental authorities were even forced to set up official brothels to reduce the prevalence of sexually transmitted diseases among the ranks. Acts of ill discipline such as inter-regimental fights and petty theft faced swift and harsh penalties with many small offences punishable by flogging.

While the serving conditions for officers were significantly better than those of the private soldier, their military capabilities were often suspect. With indifferent pay, most officer recruits came from

A Typical British Soldier: Private Samuel Wassall VC (1856–1927)

Private Wassall's life and operational/service background was typical of many British soldiers of his time even if his achievement, being one of only three winners of the Victoria Cross at Isandlwana, was markedly untypical. He was born into a family frequently suffering from the periodic trade depressions of the mid to late nineteenth century. He was apprenticed to a dyer before enlisting into the 80th Regiment of Foot (Staffordshire Volunteers) at Dudley on 28 November 1874, being posted one week later. The pattern of his service life thereafter reflected the ever-present dangers from disease, fatigue and ferocious enemies during constant deployment to trouble spots.

In November 1875 he was present at the Perak troubles following the murder of the governor there. Nine days later he was in Singapore itself. Once the brief fighting there was over, he then sailed to Mauritius where he survived a measles outbreak on the journey. From May 1876 to August 1878 he was heavily involved in the sporadic war against Chief Sekhukhune's Pedi tribes and growing tensions with recalcitrant Boer farmers, many of whom were angered by the 1877 Transvaal annexation.

On 22 January 1879, Private Wassall had remained in camp at Isandlwana when the main Zulu Army attacked. As the British lines collapsed, he, discarding his helmet and jacket, broke through the carnage on his Basuto pony and successfully crossed the swollen Mzinyathi River. However, his courageous decision to return, in the midst of scores of hostile pursuing Zulu, to rescue a drowning fellow soldier justly earned him his VC. At Rorke's Drift he was personally congratulated by Lord Chelmsford with the words, 'You are a lucky man to have got away'. He was gazetted on 17 June 1879 and officially decorated by Lord Wolseley at Utrecht on 11 September 1879. He was the first soldier of the 80th Regiment to win the Victoria Cross and he was the youngest recipient at that time.

After discharge from the army, like many of his colleagues, he returned to an old, declining trade, in his case that of a silk dyer. He was present at many ex-service ceremonies and attended the Buckingham Palace VC holders' garden party on 26 June 1920. He described this as 'one of the greatest experiences of my life'.

However, like many impoverished Zulu War veterans, despite a burial with full military honours, his final resting place in Barrow cemetery was left unmarked and forgotten. Only sixty-five years later, after a belated British Legion investigation, was a memorial headstone erected. (Main source: James W. Bancroft, *Zulu War VCs*)

THE 'LINKED BATTALION' SYSTEM

During the Cardwell Reforms (*c.*1881), Edward Cardwell (Secretary of State for War) decided that half of the British Army's battalions should be stationed in Britain with the other half spread throughout the empire. This led to a system of 'linked battalions' where existing two-battalion regiments were split in half or new regiments were formed from two previous regiments and then split into two battalions, one of which would be posted abroad to serve at full strength there, with its reserve regiment allowing for reinforcements. This system saw the amalgamation of many regiments, causing much controversy and consternation at the time.

the lower middle classes, often second and third sons of the landed gentry who were excluded from inheritance by the primogeniture system. Class did not ensure quality! Until as recently as 1872, the peculiar anachronistic system of 'purchase of commission' allowed posts to be bought and sold, often for as much as several thousand pounds, a system which, devoid of any meritocratic base, could result in high levels of incompetence at senior officer level.

Between 1856 and 1879, however, a number of significant reforms had improved the overall quality of army life and provided it with a more professional base. The graphic despatches of *The Times* reporter William Russell from the Crimea, which detailed horrific service conditions, had exposed many shortcomings in army administration, as had reports of the stirring medical work undertaken by Florence Nightingale. The great Cardwell reforms of 1872 created a much more professional army. The 'purchase of commission' system was abolished, as were more brutal army practices (although flogging was retained for wartime service). Closer community ties were encouraged through the 'linked battalion' system at town and county level (fully implemented in 1881). The length of service for men in the ranks was changed, and men could serve six years with the colours and six with the reserve. In the 1870s, significant numbers of new barracks were built and the provision of cookhouses soon followed. With educational reforms, the literacy levels of both private soldiers and NCOs significantly improved and this was reflected in the higher quality of, for instance, soldiers' letter writing.

Kit: The British and Colonial Forces

Equipment had also improved in the decade preceding the Anglo-Zulu War. In 1871, the army replaced the Enfield percussion rifle (maximum range 1,000 yards) with the new, much more effective, single shot Martini-Henry breech-loading rifle. Despatching a heavy .450 calibre lead bullet, the rifle was sighted up to 1,500 yards, although was most accurate at a distance between 300 and 500 yards. The bullet was literally a 'man-stopper' and, at close range, could have a terrible effect on the human body, with the potential to rip both cartilage and bone apart. The rifle action was also much easier. When the lever between the trigger guard was depressed the breech opened. A used round was then extracted and a fresh round inserted in the chamber; raising the lever then closed the breech for firing. The only disadvantage was that the heavy recoil could bruise shoulders and make firing

6. Martini-Henry rifles and ammunition box from the Zulu War period. The frequently alleged major problems with opening the multi-screw ammunition box lids as a contributory factor to the Isandlwana disaster were almost certainly exaggerated – a robust kick or blow to the panel after or even before the single main holding screw was removed would have been sufficient for access. (EY)

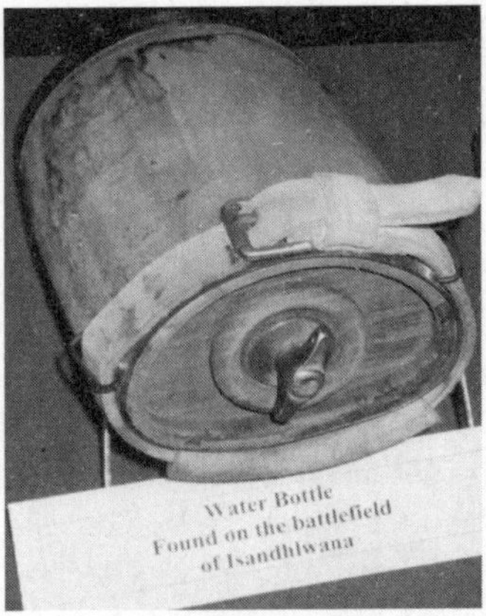

7. A 24th Regiment water bottle found on the Isandlwana battlefield. (RRWM)

uncomfortable after half an hour or so, while excessive firing could also cause the barrel to overheat, both melting the brass base of the cartridge and sometimes jamming the firing action. As we shall see, these problems did emerge during the battles at Rorke's Drift and earlier, at Isandlwana. More seasoned troops, however, learnt to counteract overheating by sowing cowhide around the barrel and stock of the Martini-Henry. The 'lunger' socket bayonet carried by most of the line regiments in 1879 dated from the 1850s, and was around 21in. long and, combined with the 4ft rifle length, gave a stabbing reach of over 6ft. As we shall see, this proved to be a distinct advantage during close-quarter combat with the Zulu. In addition to the rifle and bayonet, each soldier was issued with a standard 70 rounds when going into action. A carbine version of the Martini-Henry was adopted by the British government in April 1871 for use by cavalry. It had a 22in. barrel with a calibre of .450. A new rifle breech-loading carbine, the Swinburne-Henry, was issued to colonial troops in South Africa, e.g. the Alexandra Mounted Rifles and the Victoria Mounted Police. By contrast, officers were equipped with a variety of swords and revolvers (many with six-cylinder mechanism Navy Colts purchased in large numbers by the War Office in the 1860s and 1870s, and noted for their reliability and rapid firing). Many revolvers were made available from Messrs Tranter, Pryse, Webley and Adams, the last of which, the Model 1872, was claimed by John Adams to be exclusively adopted by Her Majesty's War Department. Other variations on equipment included sword-bayonets carried by sergeants and short swords carried by drummers.

British Field Dress

The 1871 valise Pattern Equipment proved to be reasonably efficient field dress. It included two white calf-leather pouches on each side of the waist belt, and a black leather 'expense pouch' usually positioned at the back of the belt. Other essential items for the imperial infantry of 1870s included a wooden water bottle, mess tin, great coat and haversack. The uniform was, by contrast, somewhat less practical. The traditional red tunic with facing regimental colours on cuff and collar and secured by regimental buttons was retained, while the blue serge trousers and often poor quality leather boots completed the infantry field dress. As in India, the only real concession to the African heat was the white 'foreign service' helmet displaying the regimental shako badge attached to the front. In South Africa, veterans, in order to make themselves less conspicuous to the enemy, darkened these helmets by staining, usually with tea, coffee or mud. After a few weeks of campaigning in the African bush, much of this uniform, particularly the jackets and trousers, were reduced to tatters, and often humorous-looking patchwork variations in dress took over, complimenting the wild beards sported by many of the veterans.

The 24th Foot, comprising the main units of imperial troops who fought at Isandlwana, were an interesting mixture of veterans and relatively novice soldiers. Of the two battalions of the 24th Foot, the 1/24th were the most experienced in African warfare, having arrived at the Cape as early as 1875. They had spent four successive years engaged in largely fluid short-lived skirmishes with Xhosa rebels in which the new Martini-Henry rifle had been frequently deployed, with maximum destructive effect. From the perspective of both senior military and political observers, their virtually unbroken run of success in the ninth and last Kaffir War augured well for the future. Following the decisive victory by the British and their Fingo (Fengu tribe) allies over Xhosa rebels at the Battle of Quintane (Centane), no

8. Close-up of the Martini-Henry firing mechanism. (EY)

less than the High Commissioner Sir Bartle Frere himself expressed his delight, not only in regard to the easy success of British field tactics, but also the total domination of the battlefield by the new Martini-Henry rifle:

> They seemed to have had great hopes of crushing [Captain] Upcher by enveloping his position, then of raising the Colony. They came on in four Divisions very steadily, and, in the days of Brown Bess, would certainly have closed, and being eight or ten to one, would possibly have overwhelmed our people. They held on after several shells had burst among their advanced masses but they could not live under the fire of the Martini-Henry. The 24th are old, steady shots and every bullet told, and when they broke, Carrington's Horse followed them up and made the success more decided than in any former action. It had been in many respects, a very instructive action, not only as regards the vastly increased power in our weapons and organization, but as showing the kaffir persistence in the new tactics of attacking us in the open in masses.
>
> F. Emery, *Red Soldier: Letters from the Zulu War*, p.49

Unfortunately, as the battle of Isandlwana was to so tragically demonstrate, these disparate rebel African groups could not in any way be compared to the sheer size, organisation and fighting power

African Allies of the British

Serving alongside the British regular and white colonial units were the white-officered African levies known as the Natal Native Contingent (NNC). These African troops were predominantly Zulu-speaking and members of clans closely related to the Zulu, or were refugees or descendants of refugees from Zululand. Some had old scores to settle with Cetshwayo, and most were recruited by their chiefs and headmen to assist the British regular troops and all-white colonial volunteer units. The contingent consisted of three regiments, the first with three battalions and the second and third with two battalions each. The muster strength of each battalion was around 1,000 men, and each African was issued a blanket and a red cloth headband as a distinguishing mark. Around 100 in each battalion (1 in 10) were armed with often poor quality rifles, the remainder with billhooks, or their own assegais (short stabbing spear) and shields. Despite constant drilling, their overall lack of experience and poor equipment ensured that their military value was both marginal and, as we shall see, often unpredictable.

of the Zulu, the most powerful black army in nineteenth-century sub-Saharan Africa. The potential for both Frere and Lord Chelmsford to underestimate their future Zulu enemy was later tellingly referred to by Chelmsford's successor, General Wolseley, who wrote:

> Chelmsford's easily won success in the old Colony last year was a direct cause of his ruin here as it made him underestimate his Zulu antagonists. The Kaffirs in the Koi are poor creatures when compared with the Zulus, they never act in masses or dare to attack in the open.
>
> A. Preston (ed.), *The South African Diaries of Sir Garnet Wolseley*, p.73

The British regulars were supplemented by numerous colonial irregular units. Local white-settler volunteer formations were attached to all five of Chelmsford's columns and as units for defence around the major Natal towns and settlements. Sporting a wide variety of weapons and uniform, contingents such as the Natal Mounted Police and the Buffalo Border Guard comprised a vital adjunct to Chelmsford's regular forces, especially before the arrival of massive reinforcements following the disaster at Isandlwana.

The Zulu Army in 1879

The Zulu Army, once famously described by Sir Bartle Frere as 'a nation of celibate man-slaying gladiators' owed their allegiance to King Cetshwayo Ka Mpande, who had become the Zulu paramount chief on the death of his father, Mpande, in 1872. Soon after this date, the forty-year-old Cetshwayo became ruler of some 300,000 people, most of whom inhabited the territory between the Thukela (Tugela) and Mzinyathi (Buffalo) rivers and the valley of the Phongola. By 1879, the borders of Zululand had dwindled but its social structure still closely resembled that established by Chief Shaka, the founder and 'father' of the Zulu nation. By the 1820s, Shaka, by uniting a few disparate Nguni tribal groups and introducing new fighting techniques, had, chiefly through wars and enforced integration with neighbouring tribes, created a formidable empire dominating much of south-east Africa.

In Zulu society, women and girls played a politically subservient but vitally important socio-economic role, particularly as agricultural workers and producers of food for the military. Like their male counterparts, Zulu girls were organised into *amabutho* (age sets or regiments) and only with the king's strict permission could they marry into the male *amabutho*, the latter often having to wait until at least thirty-five years of age before they were permitted to marry. In a society where cattle-raising was central to the political economy, the bride price or *ilobolo* paid by the male suitor usually consisted of a few cattle. As we have seen earlier in the context of the brutal killing of several Zulu maidens in 1876, the penalties for breaking the marriage laws were severe and uncompromising.

King Cetshwayo Ka Mpande (1832–1884)

Cetshwayo, paramount chief of the Zulu during the 1879 Anglo-Zulu War was born at emLambongweya in 1832 and was the son of Prince Mpande Ka Senzangakhona. When his father concluded an unholy alliance with the Boers in order to contest King Dingane for the Zulu throne, Cetshwayo began his slow but steady rise to power. In 1852 Cetshwayo saw his first action during a raid against the rival Swazi tribe, during which he is said to have killed his first enemy. His superior fighting skills gave him significant prestige.

After his father's death in 1872, Cetshwayo was crowned king in August 1873. The next seven years were troublesome times as he faced renewed pressures on his lands from Boer settlers and internal challenges to his royal authority.

After 1877 and the annexation of the Transvaal, Cetshwayo faced British authority, only partially alleviated by the pro-Zulu findings of the Boundary Commission. Sir Bartle Frere's perseverance with an ultimatum on 11 December 1878 precipitated a final crisis for his kingdom. He remained in a defensive posture but when the British invaded and destroyed his favourite border chief's (Sihayo's) kraal (settlement), he committed his armies to an all-out offensive.

The astonishing victory at Isandlwana was marred both by the heavy losses there (he commented 'an assegai has been thrust into the belly of the nation') and the defeats at Rorke's Drift and Nyezane.

Captured in August 1879, he was exiled to Cape Town and London where he was feted by the crowds and experienced a memorable introduction to Queen Victoria herself. Following the annexation and break up of Zululand he was allowed to return. However, after the outbreak of a civil war with rival contenders he was defeated in a surprise attack on the royal capital oNdini.

On 8 February 1884, this great Zulu leader met an ignominious end when he collapsed and died from suspected poisoning. His name remained a symbol of resistance to colonial rule and was a focal point in the great 1906 Bambatha rebellion. He is still revered today. (Main source: Greaves and Knight, *Who's Who in the Zulu War 1879*)

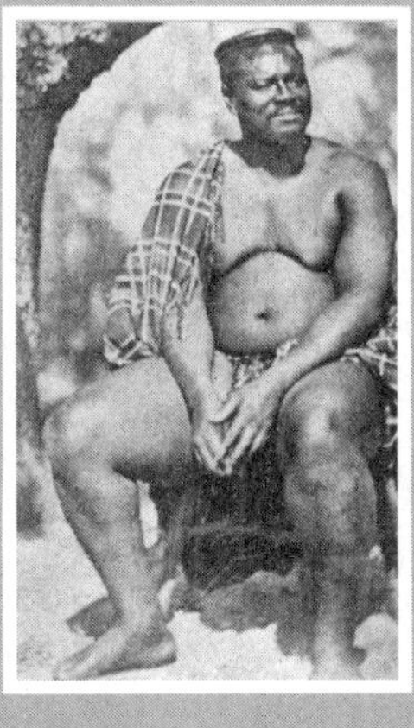

9. Chief Cetshwayo Ka Mpande in traditional dress. (JY)

THE ZULU MILITARY SYSTEM

The core of the Zulu military system originated by Chief Shaka rested upon the age-set units known as *amabutho* (singular *ibutho*). Under this system, teenage Zulu boys, generally aged between fourteen and eighteen, would firstly be assembled and concentrated at military kraals called *amakhanda* (singular *ikhanda*). Here they would be inculcated in basic military and economic skills, including cattle herding and shield and spear techniques. When sufficient numbers were gathered together at various kraals, all would be brought before the king and formally adopted into a regiment or *ibutho* with orders to build a new *ikhanda*. Those who in this way gave their political allegiance to the king were then given the right to occupy and work his land and even retain parts of the fruits of their labour. By 1879, there were twenty-seven *amakhanda* in Zululand and thirteen based on the Mahlabathini Plain surrounding Cetshwayo's capital Ulundi or oNdini. The *amabutho* would perform a number of functions or services for the king, aside from military service in major wars. These could include raiding or policing operations, such as collecting fines from offenders. By 1879, as historian Jeff Guy has pointed out (Guy, *The Destruction of the Zulu Kingdom*, p.21) the scope of some of these activities such as raiding had been severely restricted by the extension of colonial authority to the very borders of Zululand. Thus, unlike the British Army, the Zulu Army was a fully integrated part of Zulu society as a whole.

The *ibutho* were each commanded by an *induna* or commanding officer with 'one second in command and two wing officers' who commanded the right and left wings. The standard section or *amaviyo* of each *amabutho* usually comprised men of the same age group and location (this reinforced morale and cohesiveness) and were commanded by junior officers 'all of whom were of the same age as the men they commanded'. (Source: War Office, 'Precis of Information regarding Zululand', HMSO, 1885, p.87)

Kit: The Zulu

Individual Zulu regiments were mainly distinguished by their shield colouring, although some regimental differentiations had apparently been significantly diluted by the time of Cetshwayo's reign. One 'great distinction' remained, however, that between the married and unmarried regiments:

> the former… obliged to shave the crown of the head and to wear a ring made of hemp and coated with a hardened paste of gum and grease; they also carried white shields while the unmarried regiments wore their hair naturally and had coloured shields – black or reddish.
>
> War Office, Precis, p.87

For battle, Zulu warriors usually wore minimal clothing, consisting of a small loin cloth or, less frequently, some minimal ostrich feather headdress or other ornamentation.

Mobilisation for war was rapid, with the king informing the various *indunas* (commanders) by runners who then called up the *amabutho* from their specific *amakhanda* (settlement). From there, the regiments would converge and congregate at the king's kraal (homestead) at oNdini. Chelmsford's Intelligence Branch estimated the total number of Zulu regiments in 1879 was thirty-four, of whom eighteen were married and sixteen unmarried. Some of the former were comprised of men over 60 years of age so that:

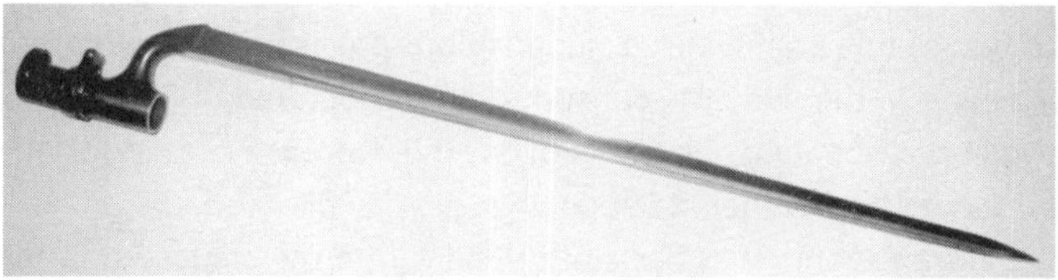

10. The formidable 'lunger' socket bayonet. (EY)

Chief Shaka

Chief Shaka was one of the most influential leaders of the Zulu nation. He is credited with bringing together many disparate tribes and amalgamating them into the Zulu kingdom, thus strengthening the Zulu polity and her army. He was a great military leader and during his reign spent much time reforming the Zulu Army. He is thought to have introduced a short, stabbing spear and heavy, cowhide shield, and he spent much time ensuring that his troops were fully trained in their uses. He also demanded rigorous exercises, drilling his troops over long distances, improving their speed and mobility, which was to be seen in later conflicts, such as Isandlwana. He instituted the age-grade system and also advocated the 'buffalo horns' formation for encircling and attacking the enemy. He remains a controversial and legendary figure in South African history.

> for practical purposes there were only 27 regiments fit to take the field whose numbers were estimated at 41,900… Of these 17,000 were between 20 and 30 years of age, 14,500 between 30 and 40, 5,900 between 40 and 50, 4,500 between 50 and 60.
>
> War Office, Precis, p.87

Important ceremonies preceded deployment for war, the regiments performing certain rituals in front of the king lasting up to two or three days. These 'superstitious practices' included ritual washing in the river, the consumption of doctored bull flesh and even ritual vomiting. On the third day the warriors were 'sprinkled' with medicine by their doctors.

Zulu weaponry was basic but deadly in terms of close-quarter fighting. By Cetshwayo's time, each warrior still carried the short, extremely sharp, broad-bladed stabbing spear (*ikilwa*), ostensibly introduced by Chief Shaka. In more recent years, this standard weapon had been supplemented by a number of throwing spears (*izijula*). Chelmsford's Intelligence Branch thus observed how:

> four or five assegais were usually carried by each man. One short and heavy bladed one was used solely for stabbing and was never parted with; the others were lighter and sometimes thrown.
>
> War Office, Precis, p.89

Spears (assegais) and cowhide for shields (*isihlangu*) were provided by the king. The spears were constructed by highly skilled Zulu blacksmiths of the Nkandla forest, or at the place of Mlaba's people in the bush country at the Umfolozi. Zulu battle practices were ruthless and uncompromising. Male prisoners were never or rarely taken, women only as booty and the objective, as in Shaka's day, was to totally annihilate the opposing enemy forces. The prevailing Zulu tactic for close-quarter battle, originated and perfected by Shaka, was to hook the opponent's shield to the left and deliver the assegai thrust to the exposed belly. Those Zulu warriors who had killed in battle were subsequently isolated in order to carry out further rituals, including the disposal of their own clothes and the wearing of the clothes of the deceased enemy (hence, as we shall see, the Zulu proclivity for acquiring the red jackets of deceased British soldiers at Isandlwana). A further essential part of this ritual was the disembowelment and evisceration of the enemy dead, a practice which horrified and enraged the British, but which was considered by the Zulu essential to prevent retribution by the enemy's spirit or future misfortune. Deserters and cowards faced the death penalty.

The Zulu armoury was supplemented by significant numbers of mostly obsolete European firearms, such as muzzle-loading Enfield 'Tower' Muskets. These were acquired mainly from Portuguese traders in the Delagoa Bay area, fuelling Sir Bartle Frere's fears of conspiratorial links between the Zulu and rival European powers. Ingenious methods were deployed to compensate for the frequent lack of modern ammunition. Thus H.L. Hall, a veteran of the

Sekhukhune campaign in the Transvaal, described the unnerving experience of being under fire from such weapons:

> The natives were armed with muzzle-loaders and flint-lock guns of very ancient makes purchased in Lourenco Marques or from traders who roamed those parts and did very good business. Their bullets were curiosities. They were very short of lead, and to spin it out they would put a stone or a bit of iron pot-leg into the bullet mould and pour the lead in. This accounted for the whizzing noise that we heard after seeing the puff of smoke. You could hear them approaching and wondered who would be hit. They were very poor shots and generally missed us, even at close range. Sometimes they were lucky, however, and that 'pot-leg ammunition', as we called it, sounded very alarming.
>
> H.L. Hall, *I Have Reaped my Mealies*

The Zulu Commanders, Tactics and Logistics

Zulu battle tactics, again based on the innovative ideas of the Zulu military genius, Shaka, hinged upon the rapid encircling and enveloping formation known as '*impondo zankomo*' ('beast's horns'). The Zulu regiments (or impis) generally comprising the young and more able-bodied *amabutho*, occupied the two fast-moving left and right wings, the 'horns' or 'claws' of the crescent-shaped mass, with the aim of rapidly surrounding the enemy on each flank. Meanwhile, a powerful body of the more experienced *amabutho*, comprising the 'chest' of the beast, would attack and distract the enemy head-on, with a reserve or 'loins' deployed behind as reinforcements. Strict discipline was paramount, the 'loins' often kept seated with their backs to the action to discourage premature intervention. Sometimes groups of very young, raw and easily excitable warriors would be deployed even further back and restricted to mopping-up operations only. Chelmsford's Intelligence Branch thus stressed how speed and duplicity were key features of this ingenious battle tactic:

A Typical Zulu Warrior

The life of a Zulu warrior was both physically extremely robust and also deeply spiritual. His entire boyhood would be focused on the veldt, usually tending cattle. This outdoor existence would toughen his body and provide him with extensive knowledge of local terrain. He would become expert in herding, hunting and fighting skills, for example learning to use the light-throwing assegai in order to hunt small game and protect his herd from predators. Walking or running over long distances of up to 40–50 miles (64–80km) was common by adulthood. His diet both as a novice and warrior would consist of at least two meals a day, with the food including boiled or toasted maize cobs, boiled sweet potatoes, served from a common food bowl shared by each member of the family. Meat was considered a luxury, especially beef, for Zulu status was measured by the number of cattle they owned. These martial skills were reinforced by complete submission to the authority of their all-powerful elders or *amakhosi*. Any deviation from unquestioning obedience could lead to a range of severe penalties including banishment or even death. At puberty the young boys were bonded together into age groups based on military kraals run by *indunas* who were responsible for order and discipline, where they were taught the elementary skills of combat. Adolescent Zulus were formed into regiments and placed in military kraals. Their essentially feudal duties could range from simple policing to all out war against the king's enemies. Injuries were treated by specialist herbalists with both physiological and psychological effects.

This intensely physical world was matched by a deeply spiritual dimension. Their ancestral spirits, *amadlozi*, kept a watchful eye, intervening to bring either good luck or disaster. Hence the importance of rituals and ceremony throughout their lives, especially the up to three-day ceremonies conducted before battle. Such intense physical virtues and deep unshakeable spiritual beliefs made the Zulu warrior a formidable enemy for the British to contend with. (Sources: Knight, *Zulu Rising* and Laband, *Rise and Fall of the Zulu Kingdom*)

11. A typical Zulu warrior. Zulu boys would be taught basic economic and military skills at military kraals, known as 'amakhanda'. (AB)

12. A classic, accurate engraving of a Zulu charge. Note the deployment of muskets alongside traditional spears and assegais. *(EY)*

> The Zulus advance in a long thick line which breaks up and approach the enemy in apparent confusion. The flanks move off rapidly to the right and left and circling round when out of sight, formed the horns or claws which gripped the enemy while the centre attacks in front from the chest.
>
> War Office, Precis, p.88

It was a formidable killing machine, especially when deployed against a demoralised, ill-disciplined, or, as we shall see at Isandlwana, complacent enemy. Zulu intelligence, transport and logistics were (like their dress, weapons and tactics), simple but extremely effective in a country comprising extremely rough terrain and intrinsically hostile to any form of wheeled transport. As a rule, the Zulu impis marched at the double, covering up to 50 miles (80km) a day on a specific campaign march. Speed and mobility were enormously enhanced by the minimal supply lines required. Chelmsford's intelligence officers were acutely aware of their efficacy:

> The Zulu army required little Commissariat or transport. Three or four days' provisions in the shape of maize or millet, and a herd of cattle proportional to the distance to be traversed, accompanied each regiment. The provisions and camp equipage which consisted of sleeping mats and blankets were carried by lads who followed each regiment and also assisted in driving the cattle.
>
> War Office, Precis, p.87

Zulu girls would also often accompany columns for short distances until the food they carried ran out. When away from the *amakhanda*, Zulu foraging parties would sometimes requisition and thereby prejudice local food supplies. One Zulu boy recollected how his *umuzi* (village) was 'visited' by one such party in early January 1879 at the start of the Isandlwana campaign. As Usutus (generic name for the people of Cetshwayo) appeared through the fog:

> they saw the many sheep belonging to our father and other people... and said, 'a bit of food for us, this, master'. They stabbed some of the sheep; they drained our calabashes, they took the [dead] sheep away with them. Suddenly one of the warriors espied an excessively fine kid. He seized it. Our father [uncle] seized it and the warriors seized it too. The next moment up came the indunas [officers] and scolded the regiment.
>
> 'A Zulu Boy's Recollection of the Zulu War', *Natalia*, December 1978

The need for long-term food supplies was a glaring weakness in the Zulu military system, as regiments had to periodically disperse in order to harvest their crops. It was a weakness fully exploited by Chelmsford's commanders later in the war. The rolling hills, deep ravines or *dongas*, and even the larger rivers, presented little obstacle to these highly mobile war impis. One source described the ingenious Zulu method of crossing swollen rivers:

> When they come to a stream in flood which is out of their depth and does not exceed from ten to fifteen yards in breadth, they

Zulu Commander: Ntshingwayo ka Mahole (*c.*1810–1883)

Ntshingwayo was the distinguished overall commander at Isandlwana. His early career remains a mystery but he was enrolled in the uDlambedlu *ibutho*. He probably served in the disastrous war against the Boer Voortrekkers in 1838 and some of the campaigns against the Swazi. Despite his support for a rival prince, Mbuyazi, in the bloody 1856 succession war, the victor, Cetshwayo, forgave his actions and he was given several prominent positions during the growing tensions and confrontations with the Transvaal Boers.

After Cetshwayo's coronation, his position was elevated due to his personal friendship with the king's new senior *induna* Mnyamana and Cetshwayo appointed him commander of the Kwa Gqikazi royal homestead and effectively Commander-in-Chief of the Zulu Army. Despite advocating a cautious policy against the British in the 1877–79 build up to war, he regretfully accepted the inevitability of armed resistance when faced with the uncompromising British ultimatum.

This 70-year-old grey-haired, stocky and powerful man demonstrated a commanding presence and his strategic ability, authority and charisma played a key role in the stunning Zulu victory at Isandlwana. He cleverly deployed and hid the main Zulu Army in the Ngwebeni Valley on 21 January, and carried out brilliant diversions and feints to confuse the British. From his commanding position on the edge of the iNyoni escarpment, he skilfully controlled the battle via numerous runners. His inspired personal and direct intervention to rouse the uKhandempemvu Regiment as the attack stalled under British volley fire proved critical. He paid a heavy personal price as two of his sons were seriously wounded during the battle.

His next major role was in command of the Zulu Army at Khambula, but British discipline, fire power and the ill-discipline of his younger *amabutho* fatally compromised his tactics. His final major role was at the battle of oNdini on 4 July 1879, where Cetshwayo's Zulu impis were irrevocably and finally broken by Chelmsford's massed and vastly superior fire power. During Cetshwayo's subsequent exile he remained loyal to the Royal House. However, his final command in the tragic civil war following Cetshwayo's return proved disastrous. His surprised and disorganised forces were overwhelmed by rival Zibhebu's regiments at oNdini on 21 July 1883 and the elderly chief was himself overtaken and killed in the ensuing rout alongside fifty other elderly retainers. His body was never found, and so perished one of the greatest Zulu commanders. (Source: Greaves and Knight, *Who's Who in the Zulu War 1879*, 2, p.199)

Mavemengwana kaNdlela (1820s–1893)

Mavemengwana was one of the co-leaders directing the Zulu tactics at Isandlwana. He was born into the Nthuli clan located by the Thukela River. He was the son of Ndelela KaSompisi, a renowned warrior during King Shaka's reign.

Belonging to the same age set as Cetshwayo, he was also a personal friend of his and was attached to the amaPhela Regiment during the 1840s. He took part in several campaigns against rival tribes, notably the 1847 war with the Swazi. As a royal favourite he was given co-command of the main Zulu Army alongside Ntshingwayo after the British invasion of Zululand in 1879. This 50-year-old commander apparently harmonised well with the older and more experienced Ntshingwayo who naturally dominated the command at Isandlwana.

After the stupendous Zulu victory there he later jointly commanded the Zulu forces which were defeated at the battle of kwa Gingindlovu which ended Zulu power in the coastal sector. After directing raids into Natal, Mavemengwana finally surrendered to the British on 5 August 1879. He remained loyal to Cetshwayo after his capture and exile, on his return in 1883 and during the ensuing civil war, in which his brother was killed. This great Zulu commander died about 1893. (Source: Greaves and Knight, *Who's Who in the Zulu War 1879*, 2, p.165)

13. Zulu warrior group. (AB)

> plunge into it in a dense mass, holding on to one another, those below forcing the others forward and thus they succeed in crossing with a loss of only a few of their number.
>
> War Office, Precis, pp.87–8

For traditional and spiritual reasons Cetshwayo himself was unable to undertake direct field or active command. The Zulu high command structure largely consisted of Cetshwayo's favourite *indunas* (officers), who had previously displayed conspicuous loyalty at times of crisis, notably the bitter and bloody succession war of 1856 or in the many confrontations with the Boer enemy, or those who were closely related to his royal clan or who satisfied both criteria. The two joint commanders of his main army, which confronted Chelmsford's main No. 3 Column at Isandlwana, Mavemengwana and Ntshingwayo fulfilled one or both of these criteria.

The British Commanders, Tactics and Logistics

The initial campaign plans of Lord Chelmsford, Commander-in-Chief of the British invasion forces in January 1879, were simple. Aware of Zulu mobility, the overriding main strategic aim was to force the Zulu Army to battle by striking decisively at the enemy's centre of gravity, the Zulu capital of Ulundi (or more specifically, Cetshwayo's royal kraal or personal home at oNdini). In such a battle, superior British volley fire would, it was believed, as at the battle of Centane, irrevocably smash the exposed Zulu impis in the open field. For this purpose, Chelmsford divided his force into five columns, each mixing British regular infantry with other colonial units. Three of these would advance from widely separated points on the Zululand border with Natal, with two columns held in reserve along the border to protect local white settlers against any Zulu breakthrough. In a strange replication of Zulu tactics, these three attacking columns would be deployed in a slowly enveloping pincer movement aimed towards the Zulu capital. No. 4 Column, the northernmost on Chelmsford's left, was commanded by Colonel Charles Pearson and comprised nearly

5,000 men. The main thrust of the invasion centred on No. 3 Column, led by Colonel Richard Glyn, which comprised just under 4,700 men.

This column was accompanied by Chelmsford himself. An early decisive blow by any of these three columns was considered essential. As Chelmsford informed the Secretary of State for War:

> In conducting operations against an enemy like the Zulu the first blow struck should be a heavy one and I am satisfied that no greater mistake can be made than to conquer him with insufficient means. He has the advantage of being able to march in one day at least three times as far as the British soldier and he has no Commissariat train to help him… unless his country… is attacked by several columns and each strong enough to hold its own, moving in from different directions he has always the power to evade the blow and to prolong the war to an indefinite time.
>
> WO 33/33, Chelmsford to Secretary of State for War, 11 November 1878

Already confident of his military superiority in open battle, much of Chelmsford's pre-invasion preparations were focused on the immense logistical, supply and transport problems presented by such a difficult country lacking any form of road. In a letter to Surveyor General of Ordnance, despatched as early as August 1878, Chelmsford had painted an exceedingly bleak picture:

> Transport will be our greatest difficulty and source of expenditure – it will cost more than double the rates paid on the Eastern frontier and, at present, I see no remedy. Even advertisements for transport have failed to produce any reductions in cost.
>
> WO 33/33 Chelmsford to Surveyor General of Ordnance, August 1878

A rare memoir by H.L. Hall, a Transport Conductor earning the princely sum of ten shillings a day, reveals the extent of the transport crisis with a frantic search for bullocks, horses and even

British Commander in Chief: General Lord Chelmsford (1827–1905)

Frederick Augustus Thesiger was born on 31 May 1827 (he succeeded the title Lord Chelmsford on 5 October 1878). Educated at Eton, he purchased a commission in the Rifle Brigade. He served in the Crimea in a non-active staff duty capacity and later saw limited action in the mopping-up operations in the Indian Mutiny in 1859. He was also involved in the Abyssinian campaign of 1868 as Deputy Adjutant General. Later as the ADC to the Queen and Adjutant General of India, he met the Governor of Bombay Sir Henry Bartle Frere, a man with whose political fate he was destined to be closely entwined.

After returning to serve at Aldershot he accepted his first independent active service command in thirty-four years in South Africa in 1878. He played a key role in the final stages of the Cape-Xhosa War, remembered as a commanding, robust personality with a tall spare frame, black beard and bushy eyebrows. As a tactician he was considered competent but uninspired. In South Africa he renewed his acquaintance with Frere and fully shared his views on confederation and imperial security, for which the Zulu were perceived as a major obstacle.

On 11 January 1879 Chelmsford led the invasion of Zululand and achieved his first minor success against the stronghold of the border chief, Sihayo, the next day. After transport delays due to the terrible terrain he first reached the campsite of Isandlwana. Here, he was much criticised for failing to secure the camp defences and for allowing his forces to be divided as he left the camp in a fruitless search for the main Zulu Army. On 22 January 1879 he was consequently at least 12 miles (19km) away when his weakened garrison was destroyed. Despite the shock of a defeat and ignoring advice to retire on health grounds, he persevered with a renewed offensive in March 1879 and finally broke Cetshwayo's regiments at the Battle of Ulundi on 4 July 1879.

On his return to Britain he was vilified by the press and by government critics, including Disraeli. Despite initial misgivings, most of the military establishment rallied to his support as did Queen Victoria. He later became a full general but was significantly not trusted with a field command ever again. He continued to deny responsibility for the Isandlwana disaster until he died on 9 April 1905. He is remembered today as the man primarily responsible for one of the Victorian army's greatest military defeats. (Source: Greaves and Knight, *Who's Who in the Zulu War 1879*, 1, pp.54–60) mules with huge purchase sums offered. After initially seeing his mule teams commandeered by no less than Colonel Buller, because 'they were urgently needed for military purposes', Hall continued:

> The military authorities in Maritzburg did not want me to leave so offered me one pound a day to stay on in charge of the mule camp in Maritzburg where they had over two hundred mules with harness and wagons and no responsible head… orders for wagons and teams arrived each day and soon there were very few of the original two hundred left but more were constantly arriving.
>
> Hall, *I Have Reaped my Mealies*, p.196

Conductor Hall was not only prosperous but was also a lucky man. At the last minute, his prestigious assignment to conduct Chelmsford's own wagon and spring cart into Zululand was cancelled and taken over by a young unnamed lieutenant on the departure day, who was later 'killed at Isandlwana'. Transport was a Herculean, almost nightmarish, task. Chelmsford had to shift 1,500 tons of tents, cooking utensils, food, rifle and artillery ammunition and medical stores via 18ft ox wagons hauled by eighteen- to twenty-strong oxen or mule teams all of which were highly susceptible to sickness or accident. Lieutenant Smith-Dorrien recorded the impact of one terrible thunderstorm on his team of oxen:

> Hail was descending as big as pigeon's eggs, the thunder was deafening and the lightning blinding. On the road in front of the store stood a wagon with sixteen oxen. The trek-tow or rope, to which their yokes were attached, was a steel hawser. Suddenly there was a blinding flash and when it cleared, low and behold! Sixteen oxen stretched and lying like dead, and six of them were dead.
>
> H. Smith-Dorrien, *Memories of Forty-Eight Years' Service*, p.8

In such broken country it was rare for oxen or mules to cover more than 5 miles (8km) a day with extensive rests required if they were

British Commander: Colonel Richard Thomas Glyn (1831–1900)

Colonel Glyn was commander of both the ill-fated 1/24th Regiment and No. 3 Column. He was born in Meerut, India, on 23 December 1831. Short in stature (just 5ft 2in. tall) he was nevertheless strongly built and an expert horseman and hunter. At the age of nineteen his father purchased him a commission in the 82nd Foot. After serving in Ireland he was sent to the Crimea and from there despatched to fight in the Indian Mutiny where he took part in the relief of Lucknow in November 1857.

He purchased further promotion, culminating in the lieutenant colonelcy of the 1/24th Regiment in 1867. After a stay in Gibraltar he accompanied the 1/24th to Cape Town, South Africa. In 1875 he and his regiment performed a successful deterrent role in the Kimberley diamond mine disturbances and were then ordered to the Transkei where he excelled himself fighting in the Ninth Cape Frontier War.

In 1878 the 1/24th were ordered to proceed to Natal to prepare for the invasion of Zululand. His relationship with fellow and rival staff officers, notably Clery and Crealock and with Chelmsford in his position as Commander of No. 3 Column was often fraught. His proposal to fortify the Isandlwana campsite was again rejected by Chelmsford on practical grounds. Glyn accompanied Chelmsford on his departure from the camp on 22 January 1879 and was deeply traumatised by what followed. Glyn was largely (and most historians agree, unfairly) blamed by Chelmsford for causing the disaster.

Glyn went on to serve in the second invasion as Commander of the First Infantry Brigade. He was present at the final defeat of Cetshwayo's main Zulu Army on 4 July 1879. In May 1880, on his return to Britain, Glyn relinquished his command of the 1/24th Regiment and took charge of the regimental depot at Brecon. Unlike most of his senior contemporaries who were present at Isandlwana the disaster there appears to have left him a broken man and, after seeing off his old regiment to fight the Boers in 1899, he died on 21 November 1900. (Source: Greaves and Knight, *Who's Who in the Zulu War 1879*, vol. 1, pp.104–09)

14. Colonel R.T. Glyn. (RRWM)

deployed for more than eight hours a day. To find oxen for the several hundred wagons needed for his three attacking columns, Chelmsford was eventually forced to buy, borrow or hire two-thirds of all Cape Colony's wagon teams. There was consequently a massive price inflation, matched by a mounting death toll among the oxen who were frequently confined to disease-ridden pasturage during the long weeks it took to build up supplies. Even as late as January 1879, as the campaign commenced, one-third of the animal transport was being lost monthly, and in desperation Chelmsford was forced to turn to mule transport.

THE DAYS BEFORE BATTLE

Policy Reversal: an Imperial Betrayal?

As the British military build-up intensified, Frere suddenly received, on 5 October 1878, a bombshell telegram from Hicks Beach which effectively reversed his Zulu policy and vetoed any prospect of a Zulu war. In one astounding sentence, Hicks Beach declared: 'I am led to think [with] the information before me that there could still be a good chance of avoiding war with the Zulus'.

Further confirmation and amplification of the Cabinet decision to veto a Zulu war arrived in another telegram of 12 October, and in an official despatch of 17 October 1878. The motive lying behind this volte-face which, it can be argued, placed Frere in an impossible strategic situation, was brutally revealed in Hicks Beach's frank private letter to Frere on 10 October 1878. He reported that 'considerable exception was taken to the great expense being incurred'. Reinforcements would not be forthcoming. Hicks Beach had told Frere only part of the answer. Troubles in Europe and Asia, notably the crisis with Russia over Afghanistan, had turned the Cabinet against any diversion of resources to a Zulu war. Indeed it was perceived Russian nefarious activities in the Near East and Kabul, and the overall threat to India, the 'jewel in the Crown' of

15. The swotting of a 'Zulu wasp' by the British lion. This 1879 Punch *cartoon graphically shows that the Zulu threat was only one of several problems besetting the hard-pressed Disraeli government.*

Britain's imperial possessions, which understandably preoccupied and dominated strategic thinking in London. But it was the cost, always a restraining factor in South African affairs, which lay at the heart of Prime Minister Disraeli's motivation for his abrupt decision in early October 1878, particularly in view of the chronic trade depression at home. Disraeli had earlier deprecated the heavy expenditure of Carnarvon (or 'Twitters' as he preferred to call him), particularly after the Cape-Xhosa or Ninth Kaffir War of September 1877 to June 1878. In one letter to Lady Bradford on 27 September 1878, he had written '...if anything annoys me it is our Cape affairs... I fear a new war. Froude was bad enough and has cost us a million: this will be worse...'

'Slumbering on a volcano': Frere's Security Crisis

Valid as these reasons might have been for the dramatic reversal of policy by Disraeli and his Cabinet, they took little account of the precarious strategic crisis in South Africa and the extent to which Frere had been militarily and politically committed to a Zulu war

Disraeli and the Chronic Trade Depression

Wars, as we know today, are a costly enterprise and the pressures at home on Disraeli's governments were not conducive to launching an expensive conflict on the other side of the world. Previously, from 1850 to 1873 the British economy had seen *c.*3 per cent growth year on year. However, from 1873 onwards the economy experienced a slowdown. In 1879 *The Economist* described the situation as 'one of the most sunless and cheerless of the century'. Disraeli was balancing this downturn with another Irish potato famine and now the cloud of conflict in South Africa – in view of this a reluctance to commit troops can be appreciated. (Source: D. Murphy, R. Staton, P. Welsh-Atkins & N. Whiskerd *Britain 1815–1918*)

by mid-October 1878. Throughout the spring and summer of 1878, troops and equipment had been slowly moved up to the Transvaal and Natal borders, a policy of strength fully supported, as we have seen, by Hicks Beach and the Colonial Office. By this time, Chelmsford had also drawn up plans for a Zulu campaign and, by the end of October, reported to the Secretary of State for War reciprocal hostile Zulu activity: 'the assembly of a large number of Zulu regiments at the King's Kraal… which… must undoubtedly be considered as a menace either to Natal or to the Transvaal.' Natal – with scattered European communities of no more than 25,000 people, as well as a resident population of 300,000 Africans, of whom two-thirds were Zulu refugees – was extremely vulnerable.

Two other strategic factors were unavoidable for both Frere and his military and political advisers. Firstly, the extreme mobility of the enemy promised a full-scale attack without warning, dangers of which Frere was acutely aware of from his Indian Mutiny experience, when several British garrisons, notably at Delhi and Cawnpore, were

Indian Mutiny

Otherwise known as the Indian Rebellion of 1857, or to Indian nationalist historians, the First War of Independence, the Indian Mutiny saw an uprising of *sepoys* (Indian soldiers) against their East India Company officers. This revolt led to civilian rebellions in other parts of northern India and shocked the empire and those back home in Britain, by directly threatening 'the jewel in the [imperial] Crown'.

massacred. Moreover, recent South African history provided glaring examples of such potential catastrophe. Only four decades earlier the Cape Governor, Sir Benjamin D'Urban, had his New Year's Eve dinner ruined by news of wholesale massacres of scores of European settlers by up to 10,000 African assailants who had swept across the border. The Zulu had also demonstrated such surprise tactics when, for instance, in 1838, they overwhelmed the Boer main *laager* (fort) at Weenen and massacred men, women and children alike. Moreover, Frere had only a few thousand regular troops to defend hundreds of miles of frontier which, after April 1877, included the Transvaal–Zulu border. The Natal front alone was 200 miles (321km) long. Defensive war was impossible – a pre-emptive strike or preventive war was, in Frere's view, absolutely essential. One other key strategic factor demanded immediate action – the condition of the Tugela and Buffalo rivers. After January 1879, the rivers would be fordable, thus making Natal highly vulnerable to a sudden Zulu attack.

A third factor which convinced Frere of the necessity to commence an immediate war with the Zulu, via issuing them an ultimatum, was the chronic slowness of communication. Direct telegraph communication between Britain and South Africa was not established until 25 December 1879 – until then it took several weeks for an exchange of letter and despatches, and the partial telegraph system only reduced this time by a week or so. Later critics of his policy, notably historian Dr Saul David, have argued that this technical problem enabled Frere to deliberately exceed his instructions and conceal his plans for war with the Zulu. But it can be equally argued that, because of the time delay, Frere felt obliged to act, as to have postponed action would have been fatal in view of the critical strategic situation by December 1879. As he later put it to Hicks Beach: 'a full explanation… would have involved four or five months' delay. I felt quite sure we could not have kept the peace here as long'.

There was one other major strategic factor. Faced with increasing Boer discontent in the Transvaal over the British annexation and a potential war, Frere felt that in order to avoid a 'two-front war', the Zulu question must be settled first (especially as one of the principal Boer demands had always been a containment of the Zulu menace; a swift resolution might yet appease them). In a letter to Hicks Beach, Frere thus stressed that postponement of the Zulu problem could result in an immediate Boer rebellion, which, by tying down resources, would leave Natal open to Zulu attack, or perhaps, even worse, a war with the Boers with the Zulu allied with the British against their hated Boer enemy. As Frere put it:

> Such Zulu allies would have been worse for us than a Zulu inroad into Natal – it was a simple solution 'risking a Zulu war at once or incurring the risk of still worse – a Zulu war a few months later, preceded by a Boer rebellion'.
>
> St Aldwyn/Hicks Beach papers, 25 April 1879

It was an opinion fully shared by Shepstone, who had already cynically abandoned Cetshwayo in favour of his Transvaal Boer constituents.

Government Vacillation

Hicks Beach continued to pursue a weak and indecisive policy, in one despatch assuring Disraeli of 'throwing as much cold water as possible upon… evident expectation of a Zulu war', and in another, agreeing to send reinforcements so as to 'avoid blame' for 'not supporting him [Frere]'.

16. The perils of campaigning in Zululand, Punch, *August 1879.*

Further border incidents (fully communicated to Hicks Beach and the Colonial Office), notably the kidnapping of two European surveyors by the Zulu on the Tugela River and Zulu threats against German settlers at Luneburg in the Transvaal, spurred Frere on to the brink of war. By the end of October, he reiterated 'the time for verbal discussion and diplomatic argument has passed'. By mid-November there was a distinct shift of approach in the Colonial Office. Before news of Frere's ultimatum had arrived, probably influenced by the news of these serious border incidents, one official, Pearson, minuted strongly in favour of Frere's war policy: 'I cannot help feeling that there could be a very grave danger in any peace arranged with Cetewayo [Cetshwayo] which would leave his power untouched'. Sharing Frere's strategic worries he continued:

> I cannot but believe that now when we have the opportunity the action which will in the end be best for all interests, whether Imperial or Colonial, European or native, finally or otherwise, will be to enforce such terms upon Cetewayo [Cetshwayo] as would at least render him less threatening in the future.
>
> CO 498/487, Pearson Minute to Herbert, 16 November 1878

Again, Pearson's senior, Herbert, Under Secretary for the Colonial Office and the most experienced 'South African' official, also gave strong support, scribbling on one of Chelmsford's despatches the critical military situation: 'the position is no doubt a difficult one and an invasion of Zululand may not be very economical of time and money but necessary for safety'. In January, before receiving news of outbreak of war, Herbert also wrote:

> Sir Bartle Frere is evidently convinced that war cannot be avoided and it could be dangerous rather than advantageous to evade or postpone such a permanent settlement with the Zulus... and I fear it must be admitted that Sir Bartle Frere has good grounds for insisting that the Zulus will not keep quiet any longer and should not be allowed to attack us when less prepared than we now are.
>
> CO 48/487, Herbert Note, 17 January 1879

The strong support from local leading colonial officials in South Africa (Bulwer and Shepstone, as well as men such as Mr Brownlee – a former 'native affairs minister' of Cape Colony), undoubtedly influenced the Colonial Office's growing support for Frere – again a contradiction in imperial policy and of the veto on war. The general support of Bishop Colenso of Natal, later a fierce critic of the Zulu War which he described as 'the most enormous piece of wickedness', eventually converted the one remaining war critic among the six South African officials in the Colonial Office. Mr Edward Fairfield thus minuted:

> The adherence of the Bishop to the view that the military system of Cetshwayo and the compulsory celibacy established by law ought to be broken down is extremely important for Sir Bartle Frere or anyone wishing to take up his defence.
>
> CO 48/487, Fairfield Minute, 10 March 1879

Recording that in 1874 Bishop Colenso travelled right across the world to protest about the injustice done by the Natal government to Chiefs Langelibilile and Patili, he stressed 'if he now acquiesces in the main policy of Sir Bartle Frere his adhesion is a much telling event in the controversy'.

The Hicks Beach U-Turn

Astonishingly, between October 1878 and early January 1879, even Hicks Beach suddenly experienced a similar 'road to Damascus' conversion. Practically ignoring or conveniently not remembering Frere's earlier despatches on the critical political and strategic situation, he greeted the news of Frere's ultimatum to the Zulu on 7 November as 'constituting proposals which I do not understand... nor do I at present see the necessity for an ultimatum'. Hicks Beach continued on 11 December 1878: 'we entirely deprecate the idea of entering on a Zulu war in order to settle the Zulu Question.' Within a month, however, before news of war had even arrived, and as supportive memoranda flooded in from South Africa for Frere's policies, Hicks Beach distinctly changed his tune. Reporting to Disraeli that Frere and Chelmsford 'seemed confident' and the 'Zulus divided and passive', Hicks Beach was persuaded to support the prospect of a seemingly short, cheap and, therefore politically acceptable, war. Frere was now to be judged not on his political principles, but on the government's political expediency. As Hicks Beach put it in the same crucial letter to Disraeli, 'there is I hope a good prospect of the war being short and successful like the Afghan campaign' but that such support was conditional upon military success was, however, made abundantly clear in one crucial sentence:

> So that on the whole, although Frere's policy especially in the matter of cost, is extremely inconvenient to us at the moment I am sanguine as to its success and think we shall be able without much difficulty to defend its principles here.
>
> St Aldwyn/Hicks Beach papers, Hicks Beach to Disraeli, 13 January 1879

Frere's political fortunes would now rest on the ability of his military subordinates 'to finish off the affair easily and quickly'. As we shall see, the terrible disaster at Isandlwana, nine days later, was to change all of this and reveal the underlying hypocrisy of Hicks Beach and other members of Her Majesty's government.

Ultimatum: Frere Exceeds his Instructions

If Frere was fast becoming a victim of the machinations of the imperial metropole, the ultimate tragic victims were clearly going to be Cetshwayo and the Zulu nation. The terms of Frere's thirty-day ultimatum delivered to Cetshwayo's *indunas* on 11 December 1878, beside the 'Ultimatum Tree' on the banks of the Tugela River, were predictably impossible to comply to without destroying the very foundations of Zulu society. Two demands in particular struck at the political, social and economic heart of Zulu polity – one calling for the immediate dismantlement of the Zulu military system, and the other for complete submission to British 'supervision'. Both effectively signified the end of Zulu independence.

Cetshwayo's predictable resistance to such devastating proposals was probably stiffened by ominous signs of internal crisis within his own kingdom. By 1879, Cetshwayo was a leader under pressure, encircled by white colonial rule and betrayed by his erstwhile friends, Bulwer and Shepstone. It is probable also that further north, in Swaziland, small but significant numbers of young Zulu males were crossing the Transvaal–Natal borders, tempted by the cash wages available in the mines and farms, a tendency that would clearly ultimately undermine the highly centralised and militarised Zulu state. The earlier 1876 killings of Zulu maidens as a punishment for marrying into traditional celibate regiments, and the 1878 border incident, when two women were murdered, may also have been indicative of growing social stresses within the hitherto tightly controlled Zulu nation. Even Frere, determined as he was to break Zulu power, empathised with Cetshwayo's deep and impossible predicament:

Ultimatum Tree

John Shepstone, Acting Secretary for Native Affairs met with Cetshwayo's *indunas* on 11 December 1878 in the shade of a sycamore fig tree and delivered Frere's ultimatum to the Zulu king. The ultimatum detailed a number of requests: notably that Mehlokazulu, his brother, and other prominent *indunas* who had violated Natal territory be surrendered to Natal for trial and a fine of 500 cattle be paid; 100 cattle be paid for the outrage on the surveyor and a further 500 for contempt if the brothers were not surrendered; also that Umbleni and his associates be surrendered; that the Zulu Army be disbanded and only mobilised on British authority; all criminals be given a fair trial; British residents be received at the Zulu royal kraal; missionaries be allowed to return to their mission stations and no missionary to be expelled from Zululand without British permission. The original tree under which these demands were given out was demolished during a cyclone in 1987, however a new tree and memorial were erected and can be visited today.

> He is now wholly surrounded by Natal [and] the Transvaal. The Swazi, and the Portuguese and must sooner or later succumb. The only prospect was to stand and fight.
>
> Martineau, 2, Frere to Herbert, 23 December 1878, p.266

In fact, Cetshwayo adopted a passive but firm posture, similar to the one that he exhibited towards the Governor of Natal two years earlier over the issue of the murder of Zulu maidens. Then, he had remonstrated:

> Why does the Governor of Natal speak to me about my laws? Do I go to Natal and dictate to him about his laws. I shall not agree to any laws or rules from Natal and by doing so throw the great kraal which I govern into the water. My people will not listen unless they are killed; and while wanting to be friendly

> with the English I do not agree to give over my people to be governed by laws sent to me by them… Go back and tell the English that I shall now act on my own account and if they wish for me to agree… it will be seen that I will not go without having acted. Go back and tell the white man this and let him hear it well. The Governor of Natal and I are equal. He is Governor of Natal and I am Governor here.
>
> D.C.F. Moodie, *Moodie's Zulu War*, pp.7–8

Cetshwayo allowed the ultimatum to expire. His understandable act of defiance was now to cost the lives of thousands of his Zulu warriors. On 11 January 1879, with no Zulu reply and with the thirty-day ultimatum expired, the first British troops crossed over the Natal border into Zululand. War had begun.

The British Invasion

Colonel Glyn's No. 3 Column, accompanied by Commander-in-Chief Lord Chelmsford, crossed the Mzinyathi or Buffalo River on 11 January, but with its commanders possessing little or no knowledge of the whereabouts of the main Zulu Army. By contrast, long before the invasion had begun, Cetshwayo's spies had infiltrated Natal and obtained accurate information of the strengths and potential deployment of all three of Chelmsford's attacking columns.

For the tiny British garrison stationed at the Swedish mission station of Rorke's Drift (which had been hastily converted to a major supply depot and hospital), the arrival of the column had constituted an extremely busy time. The post was commanded by Major Henry Spalding, 104th Regiment. His garrison mainly comprised: eighty-odd men of B Company, 2/24th Regulars Regiment, commanded by Lieutenant Gonville Bromhead; a Royal Engineers unit commanded by Lieutenant John Rouse Merriott Chard; a Commissariat unit commanded by Senior Commissariat Officer Walter Dunne; a 200–300 contingent of white-officered Natal Native Contingent (NNC); and several other miscellaneous

17. A rare contemporary view of Rorke's Drift crossing point on the Mzinyathi (Buffalo) River. (JY)

units and individuals, including the Army Hospital Corps, commanded by Surgeon Major James Reynolds.

The crossing of the Buffalo River was, by all accounts, a most dramatic and stirring scene. In the early morning fog the red-coated British infantry were slowly ferried across on the two rickety Rorke's Drift ponts (floating bridges), the cavalry crossing in the shallows. The Natal Native Contingent presented one of the more spectacular sights. A 'truly unforgettable scene' was witnessed by Lieutenant Harford as his NNC unit crossed 'Zulu style':

> The leading company formed a double chain right across the river, leaving a pathway for the remainder to pass through. The men forming the chain clasped hands and, at the moment they entered the water, started to hum a kind of war-chant which was taken up by every Company as they passed over. The sound that this produced was like a gigantic swarm of bees buzzing about us and sufficient to scare crocodiles or anything else away… it was both a curious and a grand sight.
>
> H. Harford, *The Zulu War Journal*, pp.16–17

18. Commissariat stores on the Lower Tulega. (JY)

Another eyewitness, Lieutenant Nevill Coghill, was similarly fascinated by the NNC methods, describing them:

> ...entering the cold water which must have reached up as far as their waists and without the shouting which usually accompanies them... but with a low kind of whistle as they felt the cold water rising up their naked bodies the further they advanced into the stream.
>
> Emery, *Red Soldier*, p.72

As soon as the cavalry and 24th Regulars were across and had 'crowned the opposite ridge on the Zululand side, the remainder of the column transport train commenced their crossing'. It was a foretaste of the enormous logistical problems yet to come. Captain Hallam Parr recalled this onerous task as 'weary work... wagons had to be brought down as near the pont as possible, the oxen out-spanned and driven round to the shallows to wade and swim across while the wagon was pushed on to the pont by hand'.

As the fog lifted on the Zulu side, 'a very pretty sight presented itself as the troops were dotted about over the rolling heights in

19. Lord Chelmsford, pictured after the Zulu War. (JY)

"Receive cavalry" square formation showing up distinctly in the clear atmosphere'. Horsemen galloped through and among them linking up to form scouting and looting parties. In the cynical words of a *Natal Times* journalist, the 'despoiling of the Egyptians had begun – herds of Zulu cattle and sheep were swiftly rounded up and, I do not doubt that two thirds of the fine imposed on the Zulu King were captured by the Frontier Light Horse who are adept at stripping the country of cattle'. The crossing was unopposed – it seemed to augur well for the future; very few Zulus were to be seen.

Skirmish at Sihayo's Kraal (12 January 1879)

Within 24 hours of the crossing, Chelmsford's No. 3 Column tasted its first blood. Four miles (6km) from the river in the Bashee (or Batshe) Valley, a reconnaissance force under Major John Dartnell located Chief Sihayo's homestead, Sokhexe, buried deep in the rocky fastness. It was an appropriate first target for the British in view of the earlier border incursions by the chief's sons, which they considered had contributed to the outbreak of war. Chief Sihayo himself was absent at oNdini but here, for the first time, the column experienced determined Zulu defiance and resistance. From the surrounding rocks and caves of this Zulu stronghold sporadic shots were fired, accompanied by taunts such as, 'what were we doing riding down along here' and 'we had better try and come up'.

It was a brief but bitter skirmish, with the first ragged Zulu volley killing or wounding several NNC attackers. As the imperial cavalry charged the hill from the east, the veteran 24th Regulars closed in for the kill. Once again, as at the Battle of Centane, the volley fire of the new Martini-Henry rifle proved decisive. Thus Lieutenant Harford, heroically immersed in close-quarter fighting from boulder to boulder, testified to its deadly effects. He saw 'several dead Zulus' hanging from the main cave, and 'caught in the monkey-rope creepers and bits of bush… later on I learnt that a Company of the 24th Regiment had been firing at this particular cave for some time'.

Among the first Zulu to die was one of Sihayo's sons. Once the 24th Regulars had secured a foothold position overlooking the main cave the stronghold was quickly and successfully stormed – by 9am the fighting was over. Hallam Parr recorded losses of two NNC killed and one officer, one NCO and twelve NNC wounded compared to up to forty Zulu dead. It was a relatively easy, perhaps too easy, first victory for No. 3 Column, and one considerably sweetened by the capture of over 300 head of cattle, twenty horses and many goats and sheep.

According to at least two contemporary eyewitnesses, this Zulu humiliation and small, but decisive, British victory had major implications for Cetshwayo's future strategy and for the subsequent battle at Isandlwana ten days later. Until the Sihayo skirmish on 12 January 1879, Cetshwayo's projected strategy had certainly been relatively passive, one of limited but active defence accompanied by attempts at conciliation (including the sending of some cattle as compensation for Sihayo's alleged border violations). It was a policy merely of hit-and-run tactics with the preferred aim of picking off isolated columns and hopefully inflicting severe enough casualties to encourage a British withdrawal. The humiliation of his close ally Chief Sihayo, however, was apparently a watershed event encouraging a much more belligerent posture. Thus Lieutenant Coghill's last letter, written to his mother on 18 January 1879, reported receiving:

> ...information that as soon as Cetshwayo heard that we had burnt Sihayo's *kraal* that he despatched four regiments to wipe out the disgrace... According to tradition, Zulu tactics are to attack in 'the horns of the morning' i.e. when the tops of the horns of the cattle in the *kraals* are just discernible from the general mass against the sky.
>
> Emery, *Red Soldier*, pp.74–5

His evidence is heavily corroborated by Hallam Parr. After interviewing a Zulu of the uNokhenke Regiment, present at the king's final pre-war gathering, he gave evidence that the Sihayo engagement had 'greatly enraged the Zulu King', who:

> ...immediately on receiving news of destruction of the kraal of one of his favourite captains, gave orders for the formation of the forces which were to eat up the English columns.

According to custom, the king reviewed them before they left, so that they might hear his last words:

> I am sending you against the white man, the white man who has invaded Zululand and driven away your cattle. You are to go against the column at Ishyane [Rorke's Drift] and drive it back into Natal, and if the river will allow, follow it into Natal and go on up the Drakensburg.
>
> H.A. Hallam Parr, *Sketch of the Zulu and Kafir Wars*, pp.184–85

As historian Ian Knight has recently concurred:

> The attack on Sihayo's homestead had seen the last vestige of King Cetshwayo's hope of reaching any settlement with the British disappear… his forces now prepared for all-out war.
>
> Knight, *Zulu Rising*, p.235

This change to a more aggressive posture now conveniently and somewhat ironically, fulfilled Chelmsford's own earlier intelligence reports of Cetshwayo's aggressive intentions. In one memo, written on 8 January 1879, Chelmsford had written: 'all the reports which reach me tend to show that the Zulus intend, if possible, to make raids into Natal when the several columns move forward'.

The Doomed Isandlwana Campsite 20–22 January 1879

Amid these ominous intelligence reports, the column pushed on further into Zululand. Within only a mile or two, the transport situation had become critical. It was a tortuous journey – taking over a week to cover the 10 miles (16km) by wagon track to the next campsite at Isandlwana. Hallam Parr recalled that the whole column, and in particular the 24th, were 'worked hard', the worst obstacle being 'low lying bits of track on soft soil made swampy by springs and wet weather into which the heavy wagons sank axle deep'. The threat of bad weather was ever present. Earlier, Lieutenant Coghill had written:

> I may give you a notion how the mountain streams come down. A bullock-wagon was crossing a small spruit or stream with enough water to cover the soles of your boot but with steep banks. Two teams of 32 oxen were vainly struggling to drag the heavy waggon out, the wheel having stuck – when down came the river. They had *just* time to cut loose the oxen, and the wagon and everything on it was swept away into the Tugela and thence to the sea.
>
> Emery, *Red Soldier*, p.72

20. A watercolour copy of Colonel Crealock's evocative 20/21 January paintings of the Isandlwana Camp. A deceptively tranquil scene with a lone sentry and cattle lazily grazing. A few hours later it was to be the scene of a terrible massacre. (EY)

Major Francis Clery, one of Chelmsford's staff officers, was later highly critical of the general's transport arrangements. Acknowledging he would have a 'lot to say about many things that were far from perfect with this column', he stressed that the:

> most unfortunate was the utter break down of the transport branch of the Commissariat... as our transport was utterly deficient we had to wait till the 20th before we could advance.
>
> RRWM, Clery Memo, 17 February 1879

The arrangement of the No. 3 Centre Column camp beneath the ominous sphinx-like crag of Isandlwana on 20 January 1879, one of several designated staging posts on the road to oNdini (Ulundi), immediately revealed a number of defensive vulnerabilities. While it was located close to wood and water supplies, Chelmsford chose neither to entrench the camp or 'laager' (form a defensive circle) for his 100-odd wagons. At the subsequent Court of Inquiry into the Isandlwana disaster, it was pointed out that the predominantly rocky ground was unsuited for digging and that the wagons had to be kept unharnessed and mobile in order to sustain the essential 20-mile (32km) circuitous return journey between the campsite and the main supply base at Rorke's Drift. Thus logistical imperatives had already severely compromised the defensive capabilities of the Isandlwana garrison. Moreover, it was argued that both laagering and entrenchment were not justified by the designated temporary nature of the campsite. However, some of Chelmsford's officers were aware of these defensive vulnerabilities. Colonel Glyn's suggestion that the camp be laagered was rejected on the grounds of the potential time delay and the need to keep the wagons mobile for ongoing supply purposes.

The chronic defensive situation was not helped by the highly dispersed and often sprawling layout of the campsite. The camp fronted east and was partly pitched on the 'Nek' (or saddle) between a small hill and the inaccessible side of Isandlwana Crag and partly on the slopes below the crag. It was organised as follows: The 1/24th camp was situated on the right of the wagon track; on the other side of this track was most of the colonial mounted infantry and volunteer horse. Next in line was the camp of 'N' Battery of the Royal Artillery, and above and a little to the south of the Nek were the tents of Colonel Glyn and the column staff. Further to the left was the camp of the 2/24th and on the extreme left was positioned the camp of the 1st/2nd Battalion, 3rd Regiment of the NNC, whose commander Lieutenant Harford observed the ramshackle setting-up of his camp:

> Our camp was on the extreme left… just below Isandlhwana hill itself… plenty of wood being close at hand below the hill. The natives soon set to work to run up shelters for themselves… a

> queer-looking place they made of it, being packed like sardines the space allotted to them being very limited.
>
> Harford, *Zulu War Journal*, pp.22–3

The whole camp extended to about a 1,300-yard frontage, protected only to the rear by the crag and lacking any physical protection to the front or flanks. It was a potential defensive nightmare with the two ammunition wagons of the battalions positioned as much as half a mile apart. The garrison's defences were also severely compromised by the restricted use of *vedettes* (mounted sentries) and cavalry in general who, until the fateful morning of 22 January, were not deployed beyond the Nqutu Heights and were, therefore, unable to detect the arrival and concealment of the main Zulu Army. Lieutenant Melvill of the 24th Foot also expressed his deep unease over the open deployment of the camp as did several accompanying Boer scouts who were familiar with the speed and mobility of Zulu tactics. As Melvill confided to a Staff Officer:

> I know what you are thinking by your face, Sir. You are abusing the camp and you are quite right. These Zulus will charge home and, with our small numbers, we ought to be in laager or at any rate be prepared to stand shoulder to shoulder.
>
> RRWM, Historical Records of the Second Battalion 24th Regiment, Secunderabad, 1884

For Chelmsford, however, the main problem remained; how to precisely locate and bring to battle the main Zulu Army now reliably reported to have departed from the Zulu capital several days earlier. It was in obsessively trying to solve this problem that a second major tactical error was now to be committed.

Zulu Feint: The Dartnell Diversion

On 21 January a combined force of mounted men and two companies of the 3rd NNC commanded by Major John Dartnell and Commandant Rupert La Tour Lonsdale were sent out to both reconnoitre and scout for enemy activity in the Malakata and Hlazakazi hills. Their focus was 'on the Kraal of Maylan' a chief whose stronghold, some 10 miles (16km) away from Isandlwana Crag, was supposed to be of 'importance'. Lieutenant Harford was seconded to this force. He distinctly remembered hearing the news of the expedition in the tent of 2/24th officer Lieutenant Pope 'whilst looking at some of his sketches and he at mine' and, not anticipating the ensuing disaster that would follow, he 'very stupidly' took 'but a few biscuits thinking we shall be back in camp before nightfall'. In fact, it was to be 'some 56 hours or a little over two days before we got food of any sort'. During these last fateful hours, the lives of at least two of his fellow European NNC officers were saved as 'terribly disappointed at losing the chance to fight,' they were substituted by their unfortunate colleagues as they departed. Harford vividly recalled his last sight of the doomed camp on the morning of 21 January:

> As the sun rose that morning there was a very wonderful sky scene. Overhanging Isandlwana and the camp was a long, tortuous, more or less low-lying dark cloud based on the horizon, much in the same form as a trail of smoke from the funnel of a steamer and ending immediately above Isandlwana hill, which, as the sun got higher was first tinted almost blood red, then passing into ashy-brown with broad golden edges, assuming a marvellous variety of tints under the rise of the sun. And there it hung for the best part of the morning, frowning as it were over the ill fated camp. I have never forgotten it.
>
> Harford, *Zulu War Journal*, p.24

That evening, having covered at least 15 miles (24km) from the camp, Dartnell and Lonsdale spotted 'a regular swarm of Zulus… estimated to be over 1,000 men who swept down… in their horn formation', and which threatened to surround their small contingent. Consequently, an urgent message for help was sent to Chelmsford via Lieutenant Walsh, accompanied by three mounted infantry men.

21. Lieutenant Charles D'Aguilar Pope. (RRWM)

It was almost certainly the start of a Zulu deception plan and Dartnell and his subordinates, Lonsdale and Harford, had been duly and utterly deceived. As Harford later ruefully recalled, 'it had seemed evident… that we were opposed by a very large *impi* if not the whole Zulu army'. In fact, the main Zulu Army had already arrived but several miles to the north, only 5 miles (8km) from camp, and lay concealed in the Ngwebeni Valley. It was led by two of Cetshwayo's best tacticians, the Zulu Commanders Ntshingwayo and Mavemengwana.

In hindsight, Major Clery's memorandum of 17 February confirmed his misgivings about the Dartnell expedition. He had:

> …felt from the very first very much averse to this movement of sending out irregulars under commands of irregular officers amounting to half the force on a roving commission of this sort. When word came in that they were going to bivouack out, I could not help speaking strongly to Colonel Glyn on the problems of this sort of thing dragging the rest of the force into any sort of compromising enterprise that these people may get messed up in.
>
> RRWM, Clery Memo, 17 February 1879

On the arrival of Dartnell's messengers, it was in fact Major Clery himself who was tasked by Colonel Glyn to take the fateful pencilled message to the general. He recalled:

> The General's tent was close by so I roused him up. Lying on my face and hands close to his camp bed I can still remember how I read out from that crumpled piece of notepaper, written across in pencil, word after word what I just previously had such difficulty in deciphering in my own tent. The General did not hesitate much. He said, 'order the 2nd 24th 4 guns and all the mounted troops remaining, to get ready to start at daybreak'. He also added 'order up Colonel Durnford with the troops he has to reinforce the Camp'.
>
> RRWM, Clery Memo, 17 February 1879

Clery then 'went direct to each of the Commanders and gave the General's orders'. Clery's last official duty acting on behalf of Colonel Glyn was to write to 'poor Colonel Pulleine', who commanded the 1/24th officially as follows:

> ...you will be in command of the camp in the absence of Colonel Glyn – draw in your line of defence while the force with the General is out of the Camp – draw in your infantry... in conformity. Keep a wagon loaded with ammunition ready to start at once should the General's force be in need of it. Colonel Durnford has been ordered up for Rorke's Drift to reinforce the camp.
>
> I sent this to Colonel Pulleine by my own servant, and just before leaving the camp I went myself to his tent to ensure that he had got it. I saw him and again verbally repeated what he had received in writing, laying stress on the point that his mission was simply to hold and keep the camp.
>
> RRWM, Clery Memo, 17 February 1879

British Commander: Lieutenant Colonel Henry Burmester Pulleine (1838–1879)

Pulleine, Commander of the ill-fated garrison at Isandlwana, was the eldest son of Reverend Robert Pulleine. He was born in Spennithorne, Yorkshire on 12 December 1838. He was educated at Marlborough College and at the Royal Military College, Sandhurst. In 1855 he was gazetted as an ensign to the 30th Regiment, then in 1858 as a lieutenant in the 2/24th Regiment. He served in Sheffield, Aldershot and in Mauritius where he became a captain by purchase in 1860. In 1871 he transferred into the 1st Battalion as a major by purchase and was highly regarded as an administrative officer.

After serving in Gibraltar he accompanied the 1/24th to the Cape in January 1875 and in 1877 he was promoted to lieutenant colonel. During the Ninth Cape Frontier War, Pulleine was instructed to raise two irregular units, an infantry unit known as Pulleine's Rangers and the other a cavalry unit known as the Frontier Light Horse.

In 1878 after appointment as commandant of Pietermaritzburg he successfully requested to be allowed to rejoin his regiment for the impending Zulu War. He reached the No. 3 Centre Column on 17 January 1879, then encamped at Rorke's Drift. When Chelmsford marched out of Isandlwana camp on the fateful 22 January on a fruitless search for the main Zulu Army, he left Colonel Pulleine in charge, a choice presumably dictated by Pulleine's excellent practical and administrative record.

The arrival of Brevet Colonel Durnford in the camp later that morning, keen to take both his and some of Pulleine's troops on a reconnaissance of the iNyoni Heights threatened to compromise Pulleine's original orders to 'defend the camp'. Although he outranked Pulleine, Durnford apparently demurred to Pulleine's view which was strongly supported by other 1/24th officers, and left the camp without support. However, his request may (and this is debatable) have prompted Pulleine to place outlying troops onto the escarpment arguably adding to his existing overstretch. With the ensuing massive Zulu attack Pulleine deployed his troops in a defensive screen but the collapse of Durnford's stand on the right wing probably fatally undermined his final positioning. Pulleine was killed in the final stages of the battle, possibly inside or around his headquarters tent, but more likely fighting among one of the last stands of the 24th Foot on the saddle (or Nek) below Isandlwana hill. Alongside Chelmsford and Durnford his role in causing the Isandlwana disaster remains a matter of great contention. (Source: Greaves and Knight, *Who's Who in the Zulu War 1879*, 1, pp.157–59)

Dartnell's message had reached Chelmsford at around 2.30am on 22 January, and the general now made what turned out be his second fatal error which effectively split his force even further. It was a similar tactical error made barely three years earlier by one General Custer at the battle of Little Bighorn in July 1876. At approximately 4am on 22 January, Chelmsford led around half his force, six companies of the 2/24th and four out of the six 7 pounder guns, on what proved to be a fruitless mission to reinforce the beleaguered Dartnell. Only six companies, five of the 1/24th and one of the 2/24th, supported by several mounted colonial units and African NNC contingents, were left in camp under command of 41-year-old Lieutenant Colonel Henry Pulleine.

Again, as with Lieutenant Harford's earlier departure, it was to prove to be a most poignant farewell. Years later Captain Hallam Parr, like Lieutenant Harford, remained traumatised by the memories of what turned out to be their last farewells to doomed comrades:

> On looking back to that Wednesday morning how every detail seems to stand out in relief! The hurried and careless farewell to the comrades in my tent… my servant who was to leave for Natal that very morning saying when he brought my horse, 'I shall be here Sir, when you are back; the wagons are not to start today now this force is going out'. The half laughing condolences to the 1/24th as they watched the troops move out of the camp; the position of the tents and wagons serve to make striking the contrast between the departure and the return to the ill-fated camp.
>
> Hallam Parr, *Sketch*, pp.189–90

THE BATTLEFIELD: WHAT ACTUALLY HAPPENED?

> Not even on the recent battlefields of Europe, although hundreds were lying where now I only saw tens, was there a more sickening or heartrending sight. The corpses of our poor soldiers, whites and natives, lay thick upon the ground in clusters, together with the fragments of our commissariat wagons, broken and wrecked, rifled of their contents, such as flour, sugar, tea, biscuits, mealies, oats etc. The dead bodies of the men lay as they had fallen but mostly with their boots and shirts on, or, perhaps, a pair of trousers or remnants of a coat… in many instances they lay with sixty or seventy cartridges surrounding them, thus showing they had fought to the very last.
>
> C.L. Norris-Newman, *In Zululand with the British throughout the war of 1879*, pp.62–3

On Tuesday morning, 11 February 1879, Britain's newspapers brought terrible tidings from Zululand. Barely three weeks earlier, Chelmsford's camp at Isandlwana had been overrun and virtually annihilated by a massive Zulu impi. Stunned disbelief greeted this news and a profound sense of horror pervaded the normally genteel breakfast-time of countless Victorian parlours. Major General W.C.F Molyneux of the 22nd Foot was one of the many who vividly recalled the devastation of that morning:

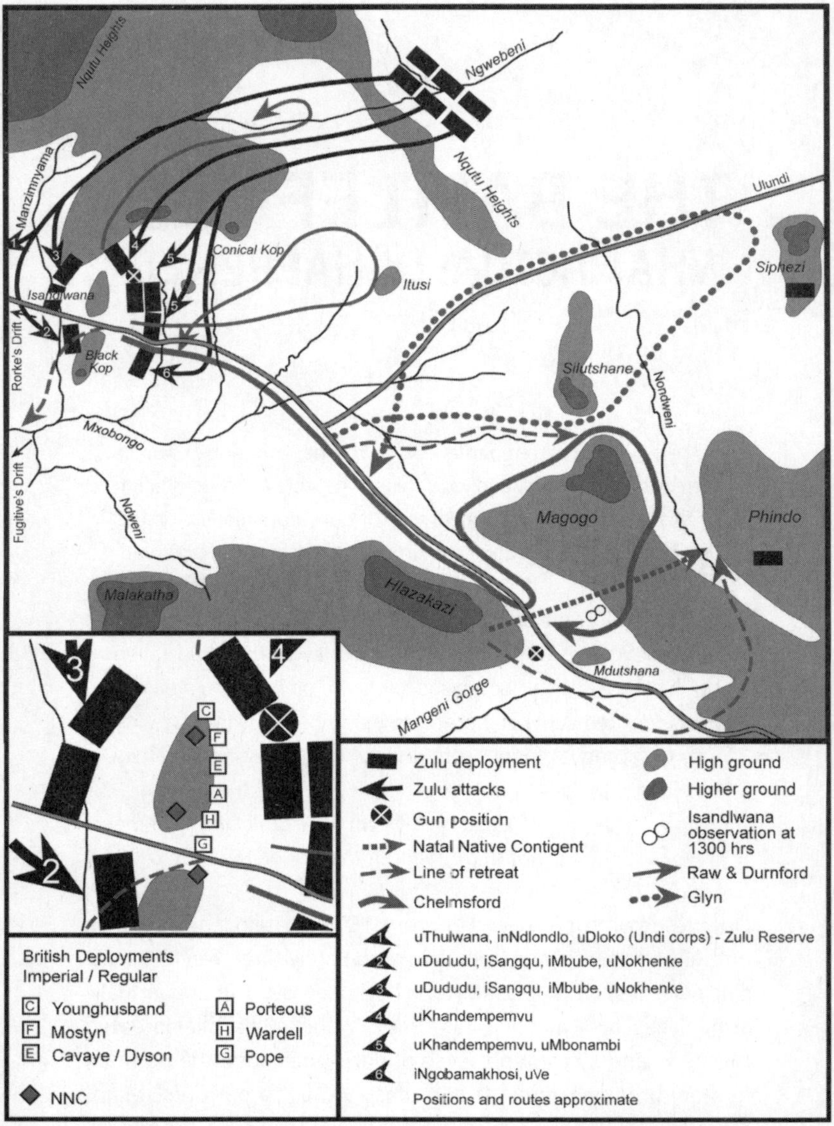

22. Map of the Isandlwana battle around 1pm.

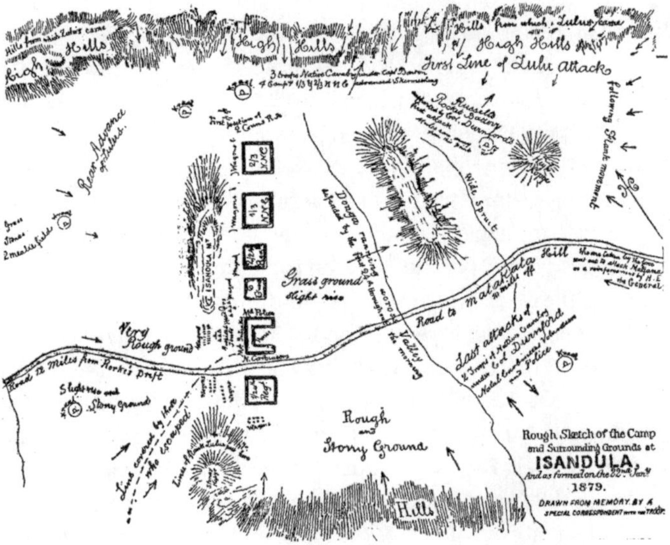

23. A rough sketch of the Isandlwana campsite. (C.L. Norris-Newman, In Zululand with the British *(Allen & Co., 1880))*

> Early on that morning my man [Private Noot of the 2nd Battalion, 24th Regiment] rushed into my room with *The Times*, 'Oh sir, the Regiment has been cut up by the Zulus and Mr Pope [who commanded Noot's company] and a lot of officers killed… the man was mad with rage. I read the account, ordered breakfast to be ready at once that I might be in Pall Mall as soon as possible. 'We will see if we can't go out together', I added and, at this the good fellow began to look less mournful.
>
> Molyneux, *Campaigning in South Africa and Egypt*, pp.112–13

Similarly, as news reached a regimental dinner held at Hay Castle, shocked fellow officers watched as Colonel Thomas, a close friend of many of the deceased 24th Foot officers, staggered from the mess, overcome with grief.

Three weeks earlier, for the sleepy garrison left behind at Isandlwana camp, so abruptly roused by the morning 'reveille bugle' on Wednesday 22 January 1879, the prospect of such a major defeat had been unthinkable. As Chelmsford's column trudged away into the night gloom there still seemed to be sufficient men and modern guns (including nearly half a million rounds of ammunition) to comfortably defend the camp against any concerted Zulu attack. The forces remaining behind on that fateful day included five companies of the 1st Battalion, 24th Foot (Warwickshire Regiment): 'A' Company, commanded by Lieutenant Francis Porteous; 'C' Company commanded by Captain Reginald Younghusband; 'E' Company commanded by Captain Charles Cavaye and Lieutenant Dyson; 'F' Company commanded by Captain William Degacher and Captain Mostyn; and 'H' Company commanded by Captain George Wardell. The sixth company of regulars, 'G' Company under Lieutenants Pope and Godwin-Austen, was the lone company from the 2nd Battalion, 24th Foot. The historian F.W.D. Jackson indicates that there was probably an additional weaker 'composite company' of eighty-odd men of the 2/24th left behind by Chelmsford. Other major contingents and units which made up the approximate 1,700-man garrison included around seventy Royal Artillery men (operating the two 7 pounder guns) and five companies of white-officered NNC infantry, several mounted African and European colonial units, e.g. the Newcastle Mounted Rifles and the Edendale Contingent.

24. Captain Reginald Younghusband, 24th Regiment. (JY)

25. An extremely rare photograph of Captain George Wardell's 1/24th H Company, annihilated at Isandlwana. (RRWM)

These were supplemented by over a hundred camp 'casuals' (grooms, servants, cooks, drivers, etc).

In order to understand this potentially complex battle, it can be conveniently divided into three stages: firstly, the opening salvos from around 8am to 12pm, secondly, the main battle from 12pm to around 1pm, and, thirdly, the climax and final moments of the battle between 1pm and 2pm.

First Contacts and Opening Salvoes

22 January

The British Army garrison at Isandlwana prepares for battle.

c.4am	Chelmsford and around half the garrison depart from camp
8.05am	Report reaches British Lieutenant Colonel Pulleine that Zulus are advancing from left front of camp
c.9am	Lieutenant Colonel Pulleine orders his men to defend the camp

22 January		
	*c.*10.30am	Colonel Durnford RE, arrives at camp and takes command
	*c.*10.30–11am	E Company (Lieutenants Dyson Cavaye) deploys 1,500 yards on extreme left of camp
	*c.*11–11.30am	Colonel Durnford and men leave camp to investigate reports of Zulu sightings to the east
	*c.*11.30am–12pm	Shepstone's officer, Lieutenant Raw, and his men discover the waiting Zulu Army, hidden in Ngwebeni Valley
		Captain Shepstone despatches messengers to warn the Isandlwana garrison
		The Zulu troops attack Shepstone and Lieutenant Raw's men and they rapidly retreat
		E Company fires on Zulu right horn (flank)
		F Company (Mostyn) and two companies of NNC are sent to support E Company, leaving a significantly reduced force at the garrison
		Artillery is also deployed 400 metres east of garrison to combat the attacking Zulu forces

With the departure of Chelmsford's column and the early morning awakening, the garrison at Isandlwana had slowly settled down to normal routine. Breakfast was prepared, the oxen and horses were fed, the night pickets were slowly relieved and work recommenced on the road. With the prospect of another restful day in camp, morale was undoubtedly high. The only hint of danger arrived in the form of a lone *vedette* who reported a Zulu presence to the north-east of the camp. The ever-thorough Lieutenant Colonel Pulleine immediately despatched a scribbled note reading 'report just come in that the Zulus are advancing in force from the left front of the camp, 8.05am'. The slow descent into one of the most tragic episodes in British military history had begun. All was still very calm in the camp area. Private Wilson of the 1/24th recalled the routine reaction to this first sighting of the Zulu Army:

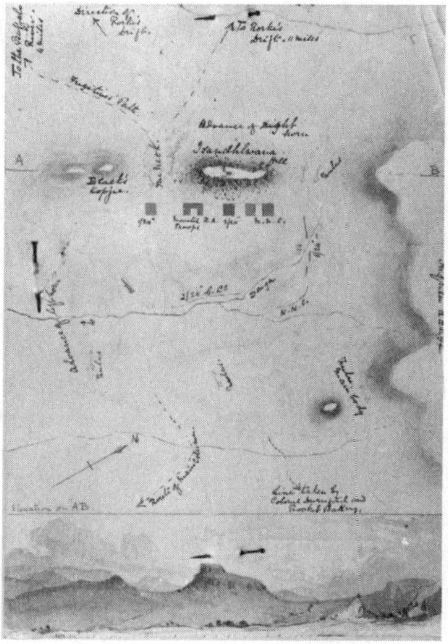

26. Lieutenant Mainwaring's sketch and watercolour of the Isandlwana Campaign. (RRWM)

> The regiment fell in about 8am the 'fall-in' going while we were at breakfast and marched to the camp of the 2/24th Regiment. The bandsmen were told off as bearers, ammunition carriers and cooks. I was one of the stretcher party which fell in with the regiment the remainder remaining in camp. The regiment remained under arms up to 10.30 or 11am when Colonel Durnford's party came in.
>
> N. Holme, *Silver Wreath: Being the 24th Regiment at Isandlwana and Rorke's Drift 1879*, p.48

Another survivor, Private J. Bickley, also of the 1/24th Regiment, recorded the scene in more detail:

> At about 7.45am on 22nd January, 1879, one of the Volunteers who had been away from camp on picket duty came in and made a report to the Commanding Officer. Immediately after this I heard Mr Melvill give the order to the Bugler to sound the 'Fall-in' and add 'Sound the column call'. Each corps fell-in in front of its

British Colonial Commander: Colonel Anthony William Durnford (1830–1879)

27. Brevet Lieutenant Colonel Anthony William Durnford (1830–79) whose aggressive tactics at Isandlwana may have fatally compromised Pulleine. (JY)

Brevet Lieutenant Colonel Durnford was one of the main British commanders at Isandlwana. He was born in 1830 and joined the Royal Engineers. He was posted to Ceylon in 1851 and also served in Malta, England, Gibraltar and Ireland. In 1871 he was posted to Cape Colony, South Africa and as Commander of Corps, Royal Engineers (CRE) in Natal in 1873. He was Chief of Staff to Lieutenant Colonel Milles during the Langalibelele Expedition in 1873 but he was blamed by local colonists for the debacle at Bushman's River Pass. He was acting Colonial Engineer for the colony of Natal from 1873–75. While there he became a legend among Natal African tribes for campaigning for justice on their behalf and he sat on the Boundary Commission in 1878. In 1878 he also raised the 7,000 strong Natal Native Contingent for Lord Chelmsford in preparation for the invasion of Zululand. He commanded the 1st Regiment NNC and he took command of No. 2 Column in December 1878. He arrived at the ill-fated Isandlwana camp on the morning of the 22 January 1879 and after failing to secure reinforcements from Colonel Pulleine, the Camp Commander, he led a small force to reconnoitre the nearby heights. Falling back in face of a massive Zulu advance he held the right wing during the battle of Isandlwana before retreating to the main camp area. He was killed in action commanding a last stand on the Nek (or saddle) of Isandlwana. Like Chelmsford and Pulleine, the other two key British commanders at Isandlwana, his role in the disaster remains controversial. (Main Source: S. Coleridge, *Life of Colonel Anthony Durnford*, forthcoming 2012).

> own camp and the picquets were then brought in, consisting of a company of each battalion of the 24th Regiment. The infantry formed up in front of an open space between the camps of the 2nd/24th Regiment and the Royal Artillery. At this time I was posted as a picquet sentry at the Officers' Mess, all the Service having fallen in with their companies. About half an hour after the column had fallen in Colonel Durnford's column marched in…
>
> Holme, *Silver Wreath*, p.46

The stage was now set for a fateful meeting between Lieutenant Colonel Durnford of the Royal Engineers, earlier ordered up from Rorke's Drift by the direct orders of Lord Chelmsford with his spearhead 500-strong mounted African colonial contingents and Pulleine, the Camp Commander. Most sources agree that Colonel Durnford, four years senior to Pulleine, took control of the camp on his arrival – Captain Edward Essex and other officers confirming later at the Court of Inquiry that he immediately 'assumed command'. Nevertheless, one eyewitness, Lieutenant Stafford, (while admittedly writing his memoirs over 60 years later), who had accompanied Durnford to Pulleine's tent, postulated 'from what I could hear an argument was taking place between Durnford and Pulleine as to who was the senior. Colonel Pulleine agreed to give way…' In any event, it was Durnford's subsequent decision-making which, most historians agree, was to play a crucial role in the fatal compromise of the garrison's tactical position. Following further reports of Zulu activity on the plateau, Durnford, after a hasty lunch with Pulleine, proposed a foray onto the Nqutu Plateau to be accompanied by a contingent from the imperial infantry. This request clearly compromised Pulleine's earlier, strict orders from Glyn via Clery to 'draw in and defend the camp' – the departure of even two companies, one-third of the imperial garrison strength, would clearly compromise this order and the overall integrity of the camp's defences. It must have been an uneasy conversation between an administratively

28. A classic recent view of the Isandlwana battlefield from the campsite, looking towards the Nqutu Plateau. The distinctive conical kopje can be clearly seen, around which the Zulu impis attacked. (EY)

cautious Lieutenant Colonel Pulleine, possessing no combat experience, and the veteran Durnford, a cavalier, colourful and adventurous Royal Engineer officer. Lieutenant William Cochrane, a crucial eyewitness of this conversation, while acknowledging that Durnford had taken over command from Colonel Pulleine, who had given him a verbal report on the state of the troops in the camp at the time, initially stood his ground on the issue of lending Durnford imperial infantry support. Cochrane reported at the inquiry that Pulleine 'stated the orders he had received viz, to defend the camp, these orders were repeated two or three times in conversation'.

Pulleine's firm stand undoubtedly reflected the considerable support he received from other 24th Regiment officers, notably Lieutenant Melvill, who remonstrated with Durnford: 'Colonel I really do not think Colonel Pulleine would be doing right to send any men out to the camp when his orders are to defend the camp'. Durnford allegedly replied: 'very well, it does not much matter, we will not take them' adding the rider that if he, 'got into difficulties he could count on Pulleine to help him out'.

29. Brevet Lieutenant Colonel Henry Burmester Pulleine (1839–79), the ill-fated commander of the Isandlwana garrison. (JY)

Sometime between 11am and 11.30am (sources vary on the timing) Durnford left the camp with his Basuto horsemen, including the Hlubi and Edendale contingents, in order to follow up the continuing reports of Zulu activity to the east. He was accompanied by the Rocket Battery under Major Broadfoot Russell and several contingents of the Natal Native Contingent (including D Company under Captain Nourse), and passed to the south of the conical *kopje* (hill). They were an ill-armed force for what awaited them on the plateau. Lieutenant Stafford duly noted that, while Durnford, 'gave orders that full ammunition was to be issued, it may be here mentioned that the Native Contingent were armed with rifles to the extent of one to every ten men, the remainder carrying assegais and shields'.

Back at camp, soon after Durnford's departure, survivor Private Wilson 1/24th recalled how the imperial regulars were ordered to fall out for lunch 'with orders not to take off our accoutrements… to get our dinners as quickly as possible and be in readiness to fall-in at any moment'. The diary of Lieutenant Pope of the 1/24th, discovered on the battlefield on 14 March, weeks after the massacre, succinctly captures the unfolding drama of that fateful morning, starting with Chelmsford's departure and abruptly ending minutes before the main Zulu Army attacked:

22nd January 1879
4am – A, C, D, E, F, H Companies of ours –
12-3 NNC – mounted troops and four guns off
Great firing
Relieved by 1-24th
Alarm
3 Columns Zulus and mounted men on hill E
Turn out
7,000 (!!!) *more* E.N.E of whom went round Lion's kop
Durnford Basutos, arrive and pursue – Rocket battery
Zulus retire everywhere
Men fall out for dinner

Moodie, *Moodie's Zulu War*, p.640

Around this time however, the beginnings of what became a fatal overextension of the camp defences had already begun. Between 10.30am and 11am, one imperial company, No. 5 or E Company under Lieutenant Charles Cavaye, was suddenly deployed outwards to a position on the spur to the extreme left of the camp, a distance of over 1,500 yards. What prompted this risky deployment literally 'out of sight of the camp' and in direct defiance of Chelmsford's orders, may never be known, but the requisite orders must have been given by Colonel Pulleine and may have either reflected a limited response to further reports of sightings 'with field glasses' of 'kaffirs on the hills to the left quite distinctly' or a belated desire by Pulleine to give at least some support to Durnford's forces on the Nqutu Plateau. Both Privates Bickley's and Williams' accounts confirm that 'No. 5 company were sent out to the left in skirmishing order to support some of the native contingent' earlier stationed on this extreme position on the Spur.

Meanwhile, on the Nqutu Heights the main Zulu impi had finally been located, but not by Chelmsford. He was now over 10 miles (16km) away from the ill-fated camp. Thus, several miles to the north of the camp, Lieutenant Raw's patrol, casually cantering across the Nqutu Plateau and half-heartedly chasing some Zulu boy herders and their cattle, stopped to peer over the edge of a concealed ravine (the Ngwebeni Valley) and were horrified to discover thousands of Zulu warriors crouched in silence in the valley bottom. The shock and surprise was mutual; the Zulu commanders, Ntshingwayo and Mavemengwana, had indeed not planned to attack Isandlwana until the next day, but once discovered, the lead elements of their impis (primarily the uKandempemvu Regiment) impetuously committed themselves to a full-scale attack on the weakened Isandlwana garrison. James Hamer, accompanying Raw and his troops, was one of the few survivors to recall this heart-stopping, indeed eerie scene:

> After going some little way we tried to capture some cattle. They dropped over a ridge… we saw the Zulus like ants in front of us – in perfect order as quiet as mice and stretched across in even lines. We estimated those we saw at 12,000.
>
> NAM, Chelmsford Papers, Hamer Account

Adopting their traditional 'buffalo horn' formation, two horns travelling right and left with their 'chest' and 'loins' bringing up the centre, the regiments raced towards Raw's and Durnford's scattered riders. Lieutenant Raw also remembered the unnerving spectacle: 'They turned and fell upon us… the whole army showing itself from below the hill and in front of where they had evidently been waiting'. These mounted men now conducted an amazingly orderly retreat, sporadically stopping to fire volleys at the oncoming warriors. Lieutenant Stafford was caught up in one of these hastily retreating groups:

> There was a force of some 2000 Zulus steadily advancing several hundred yards off. My first shot at 800 yards went over the enemy and I distinctly recollect the second shot, with my sight at 700 yards, to have got on the target.
>
> NAM, Stafford Papers

LIEUT. CHARLES WALTER CAVAYE, 24TH REGT.

30. Lieutenant Charles Walter Cavaye, 24th Regiment. (JY)

Frantic riders were deployed ahead by Raw and his commander, Captain George Shepstone, to warn both the rest of Durnford's forces on the heights, and, most importantly, Pulleine's garrison in camp. Lieutenant Scott of the Natal Carbineers on *vedette* duty over the left ridge recognised the danger. As he overtook some of the slowly retiring troopers he yelled: 'Get back to the camp immediately or you will be killed. The Zulus are in immense strength and are already encircling the camp'. The frightening spectacle had already been too much for Captain Barry's ill-armed and less mobile NNC who promptly broke and ran.

In the meantime, Pulleine's forces in the camp area had been further overextended. While Cavaye's E Company commenced heavy firing against the rapidly extending Zulu right horn cascading over the lip of the escarpment; a second company, No. 1 of F Company under Captain William Mostyn and Lieutenants Anstey and Daley, as well as two companies of NNC, had been sent in support. Pulleine had now committed one-third of his garrison to this remote position. Soon afterwards in the camp area the two 7 pounder guns, commanded by Major Stuart Smith, were rapidly deployed onto a small knoll around 400 metres to the east of the camp. They 'commenced firing', Private Williams remembered, 'on the Zulus as they came down the hills to our left and front left'. It was around 12pm – the second or main phase of the battle of Isandlwana had begun.

The Main Battle

22 January pm

The main battle commences. c.12pm onwards

Rocket Battery (under Colonel Durnford) is attacked by left horn of Zulu Army and is overwhelmed due to its vulnerable position at the foot of the escarpment

E Company and supporting F and NNC companies continue firing on Zulu right horn, inflicting casualties

E Company, etc reinforced by C Company (Younghusband) at Lieutenant Colonel Pulleine's orders, to cover their retreat

Imperial regulars force in an isolated position approx. 1 mile from camp, British lines lengthened by Zulu attacks all along the front

Zulu outflank British left wing and E, F and C Companies commence retreat to camp

Messengers arrive at garrison to report on situation across the British positions

Pulleine deploys remaining three imperial companies in camp to the left front of the garrison to protect the artillery pieces with volley fire

Battle positions temporarily stabilise on both sides; British artillery and small arms fire force Zulus to shelter behind their shields

British morale briefly remains high, despite being extended over a 1-mile front

Artillery fire control and direction becomes more erratic and less effective

It was the slow-moving Rocket Battery, commanded by Major Francis Broadfoot Russell, struggling to keep up with Durnford's contingent, which first bore the brunt of the massed Zulu attack as their left horn surged over the lip of the Nqutu Ridge. Perhaps indirectly criticising Durnford's 'gung-ho' tactics, Captain Cracroft

Nourse commanding the NNC (who were escorting the Rocket Battery) later recalled at the inquiry how Durnford, 'went too fast and left us some two miles in the rear'. Such was the speed of the Zulu envelopment that the Rocket Battery had only seconds to respond and to fire one missile before being overwhelmed. All the mule drivers and five out of the eight artillerymen lay dead and mutilated. Years later traveller Bertram Mitford met a Zulu veteran apparently injured by this one missile which had screeched overhead, showering its mainly iNgobamakhosi victims with fat yellow sparks and billowing white smoke and burning propellant. The warrior had been 'marked about the chest and shoulders as if he had been tattooed with Chinese white'. The three British survivors, 1/24th Battalion Privates Grant, Trainer and Johnson, vividly recalled the horror and panic of these moments, Johnson wrote:

> While we were getting into action the Zulus kept coming out of a kloof [ravine] on our left which the big guns had been shelling from the camp. We had time to fire our rocket when they came over the hill in masses and commenced to fire on us. As soon as they opened fire the mules carrying the rockets broke away. The Native Contingent, who were in the rear of us, after firing a few shots, ran away. I observed that a great number of them were unable to extract the empty cartridge cases after firing and I offered to do so for some of them but they would not give me their rifles.
>
> Holme, *Silver Wreath*, pp.46–7

The battery had been leaderless and highly vulnerable from the very start of the encounter. Both Grant and Trainer confirmed how Major Russell had unfortunately been killed by the very first Zulu volley, Grant noting that their exposure had been tactically fatal, 'owing to the bad position we were in at the foot of the hill'.

Elsewhere, on the extreme left, Cavaye's, Mostyn's and Dyson's companies on the Tahelanev Spur continued firing, causing significant losses to the uDududu, iSangqu and iMbube regiments of the Zulu right horn. They were reinforced by C Company

31. Lieutenant Edward 'Lucky' Essex, one of only five imperial officers who escaped from Isandlwana. (JY)

under Captain Reginald Younghusband, which had been hastily ordered in support by Pulleine. Around half of the imperial officers were now placed in a precarious position over a mile from the relative safety of the camp area and the mountain. Captain Edward Essex of the 75th Regiment (one of only five imperial regulars who survived the disaster and thereafter appropriately named 'Lucky Essex' by his colleagues), represented the only surviving key European witness to the first signs of crisis on the British left wing and the potentially fatal encirclement by the Zulu. Riding out of camp and passing Mostyn's advancing (F) company at around noon, he noted Durnford's distant retreat from the escarpment 'but did not see the enemy' and 'at the far side of the crest of the hill' found Cavaye's company with Dyson's section 'being detached about 500 yards to the left front'. All were 'in extended order engaging the enemy who was moving in similar formation towards our left, keeping at about 800 yards from our line'. As Mostyn's company plugged the gaps, the line was further prolonged 'on our right along the crest of the hill by a body of native infantry'. With undoubted misgiving, he further observed that while the enemy had made 'little progress' as regards its advance, it 'appeared to be moving at a rapid pace towards our left'. Confirmation of the British overstretch and successful Zulu outflanking on the left wing arrived a mere 'five minutes after the arrival of Captain Mostyn's company', as:

> I was informed by Lieutenant Melvill, Adjutant of the first battalion of the 24th Regiment, that a fresh body of the enemy was appearing in force in our rear and requested me to direct the left of the line… to fall back slowly, keeping up the fire. This I did… I found, however, that it had already retired.
>
> *ILN*, 17 March 1879, Isandlwana Court of Inquiry, Essex evidence

The situation was only slightly more stable in the central camp area. As Durnford's and Shepstone's riders continually rushed in from the Nqutu Plateau, bearing the increasingly ominous tidings concerning the rapidity of the Zulu advance, an undoubtedly harassed Pulleine completed his deployments of the remaining three imperial companies to the left front of the camp in order to confront the main Zulu 'chest' (consisting mainly of the uKhandempemvu and uMbonambi regiments) swarming across the ridge and heading towards the distinctive feature known as amaTutshane – the 'Conical Kopje'. The three remaining imperial companies, H Company under Captain George Wardell; A Company under Lieutenant Francis Porteous; and G Company 2/24th under Lieutenant Charlie Pope, were deployed to reinforce and protect the two artillery pieces with heavy volley fire. The firing line on the left was completed by the arrival of the undoubtedly fatigued detachments of Cavaye, Mostyn and Dyson returning from the Spur. The position to their extreme left was occupied by Captain Younghusband's C Company, arguably weakened by the inter-position of the ill-armed Natal Native horse and NNC contingents commanded by Captain Erskine, Lieutenant Walter Stafford and, possibly, returned sections of Barry's already demoralised companies. One NNC company, No. 6 Company under Captain Krohn, was kept in reserve. In these final, fixed positions the battle temporarily stabilised with the various Zulu regiments packed into their distinctive, menacing, crescent formation. All six imperial companies had now assumed the classic battle formation for defending against a hostile attack

32. View from the 24th Regiment firing line from where, behind the boulders, the Zulu advance was temporarily stemmed. (EY)

from a colonial enemy, tactics that were constantly drilled into the minds of every imperial officer and soldier at Sandhurst, Aldershot and Brecon. With the arrival of Durnford's force of roughly 200 men on the right flank, the combined volley fire from up to 1,000 Martini-Henry rifles and carbines, reinforced by shells and, ultimately, case shot from the two 7 pounder guns, ensured that most Zulu casualties occurred at this point. For a brief while it must have seemed that Chelmsford's and Pulleine's battle plans might yet come to fruition. Another survivor, Lieutenant Horace Smith-Dorrien (later to achieve fame as a commander in the British Expeditionary Force in 1914), testified to the initial steadiness of the imperial lines:

> The Zulu army… moved steadily on to where the five companies of the 24th were lying down covering the camp. They were giving vent to no loud war-cries but to a low musical murmuring noise which gave the impression of bees getting nearer and nearer. Here was a more serious matter for these brave warriors, for the regiment opposed to them were no boy recruits, but war-worn

'Blue on Blue'

Blue on blue incidents refer to 'friendly fire', where troops mistakenly fire upon their own or allied forces. The North Atlantic Treaty Organisation (NATO) devised the term, as their forces were identified by blue pennants during military exercises; the term 'friendly fire' is predominantly used by US forces. Such incidents are often due to errors of position or identification, particularly common during air or artillery strikes, when communication between units is delayed or sporadic.

> matured men mostly with beards and fresh from campaigning in the old colony where they had carried everything before them. Possessed of splendid discipline and sure of success, they lay on their position making every round tell, so much that when the Zulu Army was 400 yards off it wavered.
>
> Smith-Dorrien, *Forty-Eight Years'*, pp.13–14

While hundreds of Zulu crouched down beneath their shields in desperate and pitiful attempts to evade the merciless tirade, morale remained high among the imperial regulars. Other eyewitnesses confirmed this brief imperial domination of the battlefield as a mood of confidence, almost nonchalance, permeated through to the rank and file. James Brickhill, a column interpreter, remarked on 'the increasing gun roll' sustained by the regular infantry, with Lieutenant Essex, now returned from the Spur and positioned near the central firing line, observing the 24th Foot regulars 'laughing, chattering and even joking as they unleashed volley after volley into the dense black masses'.

It was an undoubtedly false sense of security. The imperial forces were still overextended over at least a 1-mile front, and in the words of historian D.R. Morris, defending a great deal of 'unnecessary real estate'. Behind the lines detached officers such

33. An informal group photograph of the 24th Foot officers before the outbreak of war (1878). (JY)

as Lieutenant Horace Smith-Dorrien of the 95th Regiment had rounded up camp casuals to break open ammunition boxes 'as fast as we could'. There were other ominous signs. The artillery fire sustained by N Battery Royal Artillery was, for instance, not as effective as it could have been. After initially firing 'with great effect', destroying at least one kraal and twenty-odd Zulu hidden within it, fire control and direction became less coordinated, one gun firing 'on to the Zulus coming down the ridge on our left flank and the other on to those advancing on Colonel's party to our left front'. Lieutenant Stafford volunteered other reasons for the decreasing effectiveness of the British artillery fire. He described it as 'erratic, owing to the fact that the guns had not been unlimbered and were on carriages to which the horses were harnessed – the horses were naturally excited and became unmanageable.' He even claimed to have witnessed a 'blue on blue' incident when a group of colonial volunteers commanded by

Lieutenant Roberts of Pinetown had retreated into a kraal on the ledge of the ridge only to be 'shelled by our artillery' and even that Roberts was killed 'as a result of this blunder'. An African observer, Malindi of the 2/3rd NNC also confirmed: 'I do not think the shells did much execution except one which burst in a group of Zulus'. Zulu tactics may also have reduced the overall effectiveness of the guns. Many, observing the British gunners springing back before the lanyards were pulled, apparently threw themselves down at this sight, screaming '*Umoya*' (only wind) reducing the potential casualties as the shells whistled harmlessly over their heads. In any event it was, perhaps, too much to expect that two artillery pieces should have a major impact on a rapidly advancing and dispersed enemy front, thousands of yards in extent.

The Climax and Final Moments of the Battle

22 January

The battle disintegrates into chaos and Zulus gain superiority over British forces

c.1–1.15pm	Colonel Durnford's troops on the right flank exhaust their ammunition and retreat British volley fire ceases and soldiers are recalled to garrison
c.1.15–2.30pm	Zulus descend on the garrison on all sides and British defence becomes disorganised and in places disintegrates entirely The British left flank, manned partly by NNC troops, is possibly also broken through by Zulus with nearly this entire force wiped out As Zulus penetrate the garrison, defending infantry and camp non-combatants are slaughtered The centre and centre-right imperial forces are overrun by the main body of the Zulu Army, with high losses; those who survive link-up with other disparate pockets of resistance across the battlefield

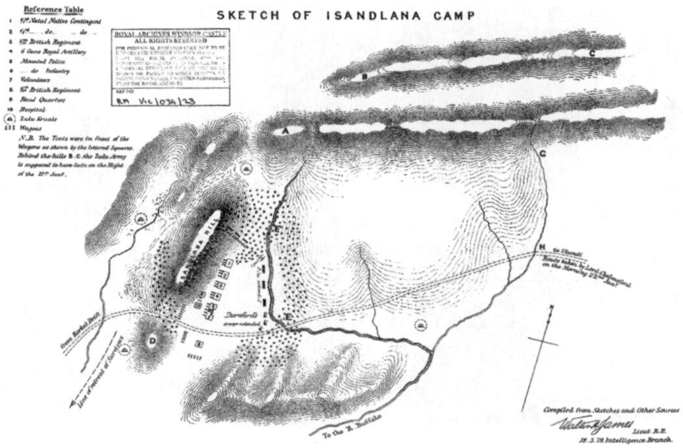

34. Sketch of Isandlwana Camp (1pm). (RA)

The isolated guns could not operate without sustained infantry support, and abruptly, at one momentous point, probably sometime between 1pm and 1.15pm, the imperial volley fire slackened and in some cases possibly stopped, as a final bugle call recalled the imperial companies to the main tented areas. Hamer remembered his decisive watershed in the battle. After returning from the plateau, he had 'then joined some soldiers in front of the camp and fired away as far as possible but we had to run as the Zulus came at us like ants on all sides'. With the imperial lines irrevocably broken and outflanked, organised resistance soon ceased. The final moments, amounting to minutes in some cases, can only be loosely pieced together from the accounts of survivors and a few Zulu eyewitnesses. For the less mobile imperial infantrymen the one certainty was death at the hands of an enemy who traditionally took no prisoners. In the words of Kumbeka Gwabe, an uKhandempemvu veteran: 'we spared no lives and did not ask for any mercy ourselves.'

What is known is that there were at least two catastrophic breaks in this clearly overextended British line. One certainly occurred on

35a. A 7 pounder gun used by Chelmsford's No. 3 Centre Column. (EY)

35b. A 7 pounder shell recovered from the Isandlwana battlefield. (RRWM)

the extreme right flank as Colonel Durnford and his men, their ammunition expended, retreated from what had been a brief but successful defence based around either the Mpofane or Nyogane *donga* (gully). Trooper Edwards recalled the dramatic moment:

> Men began to realise the hopeless position in which we were landed. Suddenly one of them shouted hoarsely, 'The Zulus are in the camp!' And they were with a vengeance. Then came the order, whipped out grimly, 'stand to your horses; retire to camp.' We all dashed for our horses, but mine had disappeared.

> I looked around with growing despair, when a quiet voice behind me said, 'Here is a horse; is it yours?' Colonel Durnford was holding it and walking close behind me. Without more ado he went back to the camp...
>
> Knight, *Zulu Rising*, pp.388–89

While Durnford may have lacked tactical judgement, his loyalty to his men and his physical courage was never in doubt.

A second break *may* have occurred on the exposed left wing due either to the collapse of the ill-armed NNC position or ammunition failure, or both. It is possible but by no means certain that Mostyn's, Cavaye's and Dyson's men were some of the first to be overrun and annihilated, maybe with not even time to fix bayonets. In the dramatic words of historian D.R. Morris: 'there was a brief flurry and F and E Companies were blotted; not a man survived'. A rare Zulu eyewitness account suggests their early and complete demise:

> The soldiers were at this time in the camp having come back from the front all but two companies which went on the hill and never returned – they were everyone of them killed.
>
> Norris-Newman, *In Zululand*, p.82

As the isolated groups of imperial infantry fought on, a confused panicking mob of whites and blacks, hopelessly entangled together, rolled back into the tented area and the wagon park on the saddle. The hundred or so 'casuals' – grooms, cooks, *Vorloopers* (drivers), etc – were hacked down without mercy. As non-combatants, their fate was in a sense more tragic than their military colleagues. Lieutenant Stafford witnessed nightmarish scenes, as:

> ...a great many of these unfortunate men were cut up by the encircling movement of the right horn which had commenced to work round to our rear and cut off any retreat by the main road of Isandhlwana.
>
> NAM, Stafford Papers

36. A good view of Isandlwana peak, looking across the saddle where the wagon park was situated. (EY)

Hamer also recalled the terrible panic, 'the scenes at the top of the camp baffled description. Oxen, yoked to wagons, mules, sheep, horses and men in the greatest confusion and wildly trying to escape'.

The remaining four imperial companies by all accounts lasted longer than their counterparts in F and E companies. An isolated Colour Sergeant Wolfe and twenty-odd men from Wardell's H Company, survived a short while in the forward line but it was Captain Younghusband's less exposed C Company

37. The ledge below Isandlwana Crag, where Younghusband and sixty-odd men made their last stand. (EY)

that undoubtedly survived the longest, as its rear and left flank was partially protected by the slopes of Isandlwana Crag. A last stand by his company consisting of around sixty men was made on the terrace or shelf overlooking the struggling mass in the camp. Probably because of his impressive stature, details of Younghusband's final moments were remembered by both sides. After being forced off the crag into the wagon park a Zulu observed his final heroic struggle:

> There was a tall man who came out of a wagon and made a stout defence, holding out for some time when we thought all the white people had been driven out of the camp. He fired in every direction and so quickly as to drive the Zulus, some in one way, some in another. At first some of the Zulus took no notice but, at last, he commanded our attention by the plucky way in which he fought and because he had killed so many. He was at last shot. All those who tried to stab him were knocked over at once, or bayoneted… when I came up he had been stripped of his upper garments. As a rule we took off the upper garment but left the trousers, but if we

38. George Vaughan Wardell. (RRWM)

> saw blood upon the garments we did not bother. I think this man was an officer; he had gaiters on but I did not see his coat. His chin was shaved; he was killed under Isandlwana hill.
>
> Norris-Newman, *In Zululand*, p.83

A second Zulu eyewitness from the uNokhenke Regiment recalls the Younghusband Company's survivors giving a shout and charging down from the ledge. There was, he observed, an *induna* (officer):

> …in front of them with a long flashing sword which he whirled around his head as he ran, it must have been made of fire Whough! [here the narrator made an expressive gesture of shading his eyes]. They killed themselves by running down for our people got above them and quite surrounded them, these and a group of white men on the Nek were the last to fall.
>
> Emery, *Red Soldier*, p.84

The 'group of white men on the Nek' was in fact a mixed group of imperial regulars and colonial volunteers, who Durnford had managed to extricate from the carnage in the camp and ally together in a last desperate attempt to both stem the Zulu advance, and prevent their right and left horns converging. Their gallant last fight was again witnessed by the Zulu veteran Mehlokazulu:

> When we had closed in we came on to a mixed party of volunteer and infantry men who had evidently been stopped by the end of our horn: they numbered about 100. They made a desperate resistance, some firing with pistols and others using swords. I repeatedly heard the word 'fire' given by someone, but we proved too many for them and killed them all where they stood. When all was over I had a look at these men and saw an officer with his arm in a sling and with a big moustache [an unmistakable description of Durnford himself] surrounded by Carbineers, soldiers and other men that I didn't know.
>
> J.S. Rothwell (compiler), 'Narrative of Field Operations', p.39

The remaining two imperial companies, under Captain Wardell and Lieutenant Pope, occupying the centre and centre right of the British lines, faced the full impact of the Zulu 'chest', comprising mainly the uKhandempemvu and possibly elements of the uMbonambi regiments, undoubtedly already incensed by their substantial losses to the early imperial volley fire. Nevertheless, they fought and died well and remnants were able either to link up with Durnford for the last stand on the saddle or, as some accounts suggest, form a small cohesive defence to the rear of the 1/24th tents (a possible third and final stand). Another Zulu recorded their final moments, bayonets fixed and fighting back to back:

> Some Zulu threw assegais at them others shot at them; but they did not get close – they avoided the bayonet, for any man who went up to stab a soldier was fixed through his throat or stomach and at once fell. Occasionally, when a Zulu was engaged in front with an assegai, another Zulu killed him from behind.
>
> Norris-Newman, *In Zululand*, p.83

The sense of impending doom must have been heightened by a partial eclipse of the sun which occurred at the height of the battle. A warrior of the uMbonambi Regiment recalled that 'the tumult and the firing was wonderful, every warrior shouted "Usutu!" as he killed anyone, and the sun got very dark like night'. Another confirmed that:

> The sun turned black in the middle of the battle: we could still see it over us, or we should have thought we had been fighting till evening. Then we got into the camp, and there was a great deal of smoke and firing. Afterwards the sun came out bright again.
>
> Emery, *Red Soldier*, p.84

Captain Hallam Parr, attached to Chelmsford's absent column but who interviewed survivors after the battle, provided graphic accounts of individual struggles. One tall man, a corporal of the 24th, killed four Zulus with his bayonet, but his weapon jammed in the throat of his last opponent and the Zulus rushed in on him. The only sailor in camp, seconded from HMS *Active* was seen, with 'his back against a wagon wheel, keeping the Zulus at bay with his cutlass' but, 'a Zulu crept behind him and stabbed him through the spokes'. One of the Natal volunteers, sick in hospital, was 'found with his back against a stone near the hospital tent' with 'nearly 100 fired cartridges around him, his bowie knife clutched in his hand'.

Others chose more desperate strategies to evade the stabbing assegais. Captain Harford recalled in his journal that he later: 'found the dead bodies of our two drivers, their faces blackened and it struck me at the time that they must have done this themselves in the hope of being able to escape'.

Few will forget the descriptions of a fleeing Band Sergeant Gamble of the 1/24th desperately importuning escaping riders for a mount as the Zulu closed in. Others may have survived by sheer luck. To his dying day, Lieutenant Smith-Dorrien was convinced that he and his four fellow imperial officers only survived the carnage because they were wearing blue patrol jackets, as

Cetshwayo had reputedly ordered that only those clad in red should be killed.

The fate of Lieutenant Colonel Pulleine, the Camp Commander, remains a mystery. One account places him among the dead at

39a. The VC Roll of Honour Board for RMA Woolwich. (AO)

39b. The VC Roll of Honour, housed in the Royal Military Academy Library, including Lieutenant Coghill, killed at Isandlwana. (AO)

Durnford's last stand, another has him shot or assegaied near or in his tent as he wrote a last letter or order, a third falling with forty-odd survivors, 800 yards to the rear of the Nek (or saddle) by the Manzinyama River. One of his last acts, however, was to entrust the safety of the Queen's Colour of the 1st Battalion to Lieutenant Melvill, who, with Lieutenant Coghill, fought his way out of the camp. Similarly, a brave but futile attempt was made to rescue the guns. As the lines broke they were hastily limbered up but many of the gunners were assegaied as they careered across the camp in front of the crag and over the saddle of Isandlwana. Lieutenant Curling of the Royal Artillery provided the main eyewitness account of their fate:

> The enemy advanced slowly without halting; when they were 400 yards off the 1st battalion of the 24th Regiment advanced about 30 yards. We remained in the same position. Major Smith returned at this time with his gun and came into action beside mine. The enemy advancing still, we began firing case, but almost immediately the infantry were ordered to retire. Before we could get away the enemy were by the guns; and I saw

40. Graves mark the site of a final rally along Fugitive's Drift. (EY)

one gunner stabbed as he was mounting on to the axle-tree box. The limber gunners did not mount, but ran after the guns. We went straight through the camp, but found the enemy in position. The gunners were all stabbed going through the camp with the exception of one or two. One of the two sergeants was also killed at this time. When we got on to the road to Rorke's Drift it was completely blocked up by the Zulus.

WO 33/33 Court of Inquiry, Curling evidence

The Flight from Isandlwana

Our flight I shall never forget; no path, no track, boulders everywhere. Our way was strewn with shields, assegais, blankets, hats, clothing of all descriptions, guns, ammunitions belts and saddles which horses had managed to kick off, revolvers and belts and I know not what else. Our stampede was composed of mules – oxen – horses and flying men all strangely inter-mingled man and beast, all apparently impressed with the danger which surrounded us.

A.F. Hattersley, *Later Annals of Natal*, pp.156–57, Brickhill account

By 2pm, resistance in the camp had virtually ceased. Those who survived the holocaust in the tented areas made a desperate dash over the Nek and along a tortuous 10-mile (16km) route to the nearest British outpost at Rorke's Drift, or further, to Helpmekaar. Their escape route was, however, almost immediately blocked by the convergence of the two Zulu 'horns' from behind the Nek, a brilliant culmination of overall Zulu strategy that day. Scores more civilians and soldiers died in further hand-to-hand combat. Lieutenant Stafford recalled the terrible scenes that confronted him as he galloped across the Nek and proceeded along the route which later became known as 'Fugitive's Drift' or Trail:

It was perfect pandemonium. The mules and pack horses and oxen, some with ghastly gashes, were galloping over the veldt

> at will, some with saddles and others only with blinkers. How sad to think what these noble animals are called upon to suffer in their masters' wars.
>
> NAM, Stafford Papers

The men and horses of the Royal Artillery dragging both 7 pounder guns behind them, and already decimated in numbers during their desperate ride through the camp area, were clearly doomed. Lieutenant Curling again later recalled their horrible demise:

> We crossed the road with the crowd, principally consisting of natives, men left in camp and civilians, and went down a steep ravine leading towards the river. The Zulus were in the middle of the crowd stabbing the men as they ran. When we had gone about 400 yards we came to a deep cut in which the guns stuck. There was, as far as I could see, only one gunner with them at this time, but they were covered with men of different corps clinging to them. The Zulus were on them almost at once and the drivers pulled off their horses…
>
> ILN, Isandlwana Court of Inquiry, Curling evidence

Recent archaeological excavations in 2000 led by Dr Tony Pollard of Glasgow University actually discovered the interred remains of these horses and their equipment.

Nearby, on the reverse slopes of Isandlwana, Captain Shepstone and several of his men were surrounded and annihilated by the Zulu right horn.

In the midst of panic there were moments of calm, indeed courageous self-sacrifice. James Hamer, by his own account one of the last four horsemen to escape the Zulu pincer movement behind the mountain, was forced to 'use our revolvers very freely for the Zulus followed us up quickly', and was placed in a 'jolly predicament' when his already fatigued horse (Dick) collapsed:

> ...completely down and would not move a step further... then (thank God) a man of the Rocket Battery galloped up with a led horse and let me have it. I had just taken the saddle off Dick when a bullet struck him dead and the poor fellow who gave me the horse had only ridden three yards when I saw him fall, killed from his horse.
>
> NAM, Chelmsford Papers, Hamer evidence

Malindi of the Natal Native Horse contingent recorded an act of exceptional self-sacrifice and generosity. As the camp defences had started to collapse

> ...our Captain now got off his horse and gave it to me, telling me to take it to the ammunition wagons and turning back... he joined the red soldiers who were firing and I never saw him again.
>
> NAM, Chelmsford Papers, Malindi evidence

Some lives were lost for less logical reasons. Trooper Charles Montague-Sparks of the Natal Mounted Police, on escaping via the officers' quarters in the camp area, 'found them untenanted' and while hesitating as to what he should do, he came across Pearce, another member of the corps 'who was a saddler and 6'6" high'. As Sparks expressed the opinion that things looked grave, Pearce cried out the words 'my oath!' and started off to retrieve his big bit which he said was in his tent. Meanwhile Sparks, seeing the red-coated men of the 24th Regiment running towards the tents with the Zulus in close pursuit shouting their slogan 'Gwas Umhlongo! Gwas Inglubi!' ('stab the white men, stab the pigs'), became much alarmed and shrieked after Pearce 'come back man and let's ride off!, we shall both be killed'. Pearce's reply was 'What a choking off I would get if the Sergeant Major sees me riding with a snaffle instead of the regulation bit'. With this remark he disappeared into the tent, which a moment later was surrounded by Zulus, and 'that was the last of Pearce'.

Of the other several vivid accounts of this nightmarish retreat, those of Lieutenants Erskine and Smith-Dorrien stand out.

Following half a mile behind Melvill and Coghill and pursued by hundreds of Zulu, Smith-Dorrien came across a wounded mounted infantryman named Macdonell. Again, in a significant act of gallantry, he applied a tourniquet with a handkerchief to stop the bleeding. Smith-Dorrien then attempted to manhandle the trooper down the gorge and was startled by a desperate shout from the white-faced and bleeding Major Stuart Smith, commander of the ill-fated gun detachment. 'Get on man, the Zulus are on top of us'. But 'in a second we were surrounded and an assegai accounted for poor Smith, and my wounded mounted infantry friend and my horse'.

Struggling across the raging 18-yard torrent of the Buffalo River, Smith-Dorrien commenced a running retreat pursued by around twenty Zulu. However, by wisely husbanding the last few rounds from his revolver, he kept them at bay. It was a miraculous escape. He finally reached Helpmekaar at sundown, having covered a dozen miles on foot in around five hours!

Lieutenant Erskine similarly experienced an amazing escape and one undoubtedly aided by his fortuitous knowledge of the Zulu language. Attached to the 3/4th Natal Native Contingent, he was helplessly carried along by the panicky retreat. Exhausted and overburdened with the ammunition which he had wisely snatched from nearby wagons, Erskine briefly rested, only to witness soldiers all around him being killed, thrown on their backs and disembowelled. With a renewed sense of urgency, he acquired a horse, and after riding about 2 miles (3km), recalled seeing:

> …a soldier who was running about ten yards from me, when, just as he had passed a bush, a Zulu sprang out and said 'Uya ngapi umlungu?' (where are you going white man?) and threw a broad bladed assegai which pierced the poor fellow between the shoulders. The poor fellow fell forward on his face and the Zulu ran up to him, calling out 'Usutu', stabbed him to the heart… The same Zulu then threw the assegai at Erskine himself, wounding him in the leg. After shaking it out

41. Lieutenant Coghill, killed along Fugitive's Drift attempting to save the Colours. (JY)

42. Lieutenant Melvill, also killed gallantly assisting Coghill and trying to save the Colours. (RRWM)

> he proceeded a further 500 yards at which point he saw 'a puff of smoke and a bullet whizzed about an inch from my nose. I shouted out to the Zulu marksman, 'Iya wa utiuya dubula bane na' (who do you think you are shooting).
>
> Moodie, *Moodie's Zulu War*, p.26

The predictably astonished Zulu let him pass. He finally negotiated the river, and like Smith-Dorrien, reached Helpmekaar in the early evening.

Lieutenants Melvill and Coghill, escorting the Queen's Colour, were not so fortunate. Struggling across the Buffalo River, they lost their horses. Drifting downstream, weak and exhausted (Coghill had injured a leg prior to the battle), they reached the opposite bank only to be run down and assegaied by around thirty Zulu in front of a large rocky outcrop, barely 100 yards above the river.

With the January rains having swollen the river to peak levels, many men who reached that far were either drowned, or,

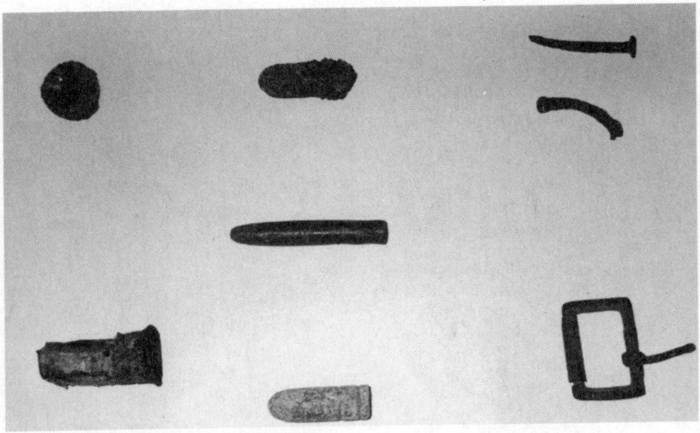

43. Relics of the Isandlwana massacre. Note the crude Zulu slug in the centre and melted brass cartridge (bottom right), presumably ejected from an over-heated Martini-Henry rifle. (EY)

exhausted, easily killed by the Zulu waiting on the other side. In the words of Captain Stafford:

> …a strange sight greeted us as we got to the edge. Men were struggling in the water. The various uniforms represented all the colours of the rainbow. Half a dozen bodies were washed ashore on the bank at the end of the river on our side.
>
> NAM, Stafford Papers

This desperate retreat was not a total disaster. Here and there, and especially around the riverbank, small groups of infantry and horsemen demonstrated great courage and discipline and thereby saved several lives. Erskine recalled the coolness and discipline of the African-mounted Edendale Contingent. After struggling to the far side of the Buffalo River alongside Captain Cochrane, he met 'the Edendale men', who:

> …told me to lie flat on my horse's neck, which I did, thinking the Zulus were going to fire at me, but was surprised to hear

> our own men firing over my head; they killed about a dozen Zulu. While watching this little skirmish I saw one of our Kaffirs brought to bay by a Zulu. After some preliminary guarding on the part of both, the Zulu stabbed our Kaffir in the shoulder; thereupon our Kaffir jumped into the air and struck his assegai to the Zulu's heart. Both of them then rolled into the river.
>
> Moodie, *Moodie's Zulu War*, p.27

Amid this carnage behind the Nek, and the chilling screams of the wounded and dying men and animals, the 4,000-strong Undi Corps which had been held in reserve, belatedly arrived 'fresh and eager for fighting'. It was clearly too late to achieve full battle honours here, but it was patently obvious to their disappointed men and commanders that only the small garrison at Rorke's Drift now stood in the way of a major incursion into the Natal colony. Their 40-year-old commander, Prince Dabulamanzi, Cetshwayo's aggressive half-brother, was an inexperienced commander but highly intelligent and also a personality. A keen horseman and an excellent shot, his ruthless political manoeuvrings had given him an artificially elevated status in the Royal Council.

An invasion of the Natal would suit this deeply ambitious man and the powerful 4,000-strong Undi Corps, comprising the crack uThulwana Regiment and the inDluyengwe, inDlondlo and uDloko *amabutho*, provided ample means to achieve this task. The seriousness of this enterprise was underlined by the actions of one Undabuko, another of the king's brothers, who even called on members of his own already decimated regiment, the uMbonambi, 'to join them but... they declined on the ground that it was necessary to return to the field of battle to attend to their wounded'. The expedition, conducted contrary to Cetshwayo's strict orders not to cross the Natal border, ended in disaster. After a 12-hour epic fight on the night of 22/23 January, the 140-man Rorke's Drift garrison successfully repulsed Dabulamanzi's regiments, inflicting over 400 Zulu casualties for a loss of only seventeen British dead.

Chelmsford's Return to Isandlwana

As the bloodied and exultant Zulus commenced a systematic sacking and looting of the camp, finishing off the last major groups of resistance by around 2pm, Chelmsford's force, bivouacked up to 12 miles away to the south-east, remained blissfully unaware of the terrible events which had unfolded in the camp that morning. Chelmsford's response to Pulleine's first message at 8.05am, reporting 'Zulus advancing in force for the left front of the camp', again demonstrated both his dangerous complacency and his overall underestimation of his Zulu enemy. He had returned the note to his senior staff officer Major Clery, without a word. When Clery asked him, 'what is to be done on this report?', Chelmsford allegedly replied, 'there is nothing to be done on that'. The failure of his naval aide, Lieutenant Berkeley Milne, to discern through his field glasses any major hostile activity in the camp area from the nearby hill, only served to enhance Chelmsford's continuing over-confidence. Colour Sergeant James Gittins 2/24th provided a rare account from the ranks of the columns' overall ignorance of the terrible events occurring at Isandlwana camp that morning and the elusiveness of their Zulu enemy:

> We were off before daylight and before 5 o' clock we had got to the place where we expected to find the enemy, but they had been too quick for us and had gone. We marched many miles but could not get in touch with them. The general decided to camp for the night and sent my own and 'F' company with four guns to select a suitable site, and meant to send back to the camp for the troops remaining behind to bring out the camp to us. We were at this time about twelve miles from Isandhlwana and could see it distinctly, each lot of tents looking like great patches of snow. We were about three miles from where we had left the general. Our attention was attracted by distant firing and, looking towards Isandhlwana [sic], we could see the two guns firing rapidly and the

44. Isandlwana campsite after the battle. The bones of men and animals lie in the foreground. (JY)

> smoke of musketry. I borrowed a pair of field glasses and could see masses of Zulus attacking the camp. When the firing ceased we thought, of course, that our people had driven them off.
>
> *The Imperial Club Magazine*, 1929, p.129, Colour Sergeant Gittins, 2/24th, Account

It wasn't until dusk, around five hours after the last survivor had escaped, that Chelmsford's stunned, exhausted and deeply dispirited force stumbled into their desolate and wrecked camp. Despite receiving other, considered to be vague, reports of action in the camp area (notably around midday from Commandant 'Maori' Hamilton-Browne commanding Chelmsford's 1/3rd NNC Battalion), Chelmsford and his staff had only received a definitive eyewitness report of the disaster early in the afternoon when all fighting had ceased. This eyewitness, Commandant Rupert Lonsdale of the 3/9th NNC, had himself only escaped death by inches. Half asleep in the heat of the early afternoon sun, riding a 'broken-kneed old crock' called 'Dot', he had returned by himself to the now-occupied camp. Thirty-two years later Lonsdale still vividly recalled the horrific scenes that greeted him:

I was very short of sleep, and awfully tired. When we were within a few miles of the camp Isandlana [sic] mountain, I asked the general [Lord Chelmsford] if I might ride on ahead, get back to camp and get a rest. This was granted, and I rode on my way. I was shot at by a couple of natives as I went on, but I thought nothing of it, as I imagined they were two of my own Swazis who had made a mistake, and I did not discover they were Zulus until later. I approached the camp we had so lately left, but being three quarters asleep did not notice anything was amiss until I was well inside it. The first thing that woke me up and put me on the *Qui vive* was a Zulu coming for me with a stabbing assegai, already red with blood in his hand. I was wide awake enough then, and on the alert in a moment. I glanced around me and became fully alive to what had taken place, and that the camp had been captured by the Zulus. I saw in a flash dead bodies of both soldiers and Zulus all over the place, tents rent in fragments, bags of flour cut open and the contents strewn about, boxes of ammunition broken, everything, in fact, smashed and done for. Last but not least, Zulus with assegais still reeking with blood sitting and wandering about in all this indescribable chaos. I saw it all in a flash, turned and fled. My horse was as tired as I was. Many Zulus, who had become alive to the fact that an enemy and a white man was among them, rushed after me yelling and firing at me. It was the most deadly, awful moment I have ever had in my life… I could only screw a very moderate canter out of my poor gee… Kafirs are uncommonly fleet of foot. It was two or three minutes before I was clear of those howling devils. It seemed to me like two or three hours. At length they all gave up the chase and I went on my way to rejoin the column… When I rode up to the General and reported what I had seen I believe he thought I was mad… I don't think I shall ever close my eyes in sleep again without seeing that yelling horde of Zulus rushing after me, brandishing their bloody spears and wondering whether my poor horse had steam enough left in him to carry me out of their reach.

Streatfield, *Reminiscences of an Old'un*, p.155–57,
Lonsdale Account

45–50. Officers who fell at Isandlwana (clockwise from top left): 45 Henry Julien Dyer. 46 James Patrick Daly. 47 George Frederick John Hodson. 48 Frederick Godwin-Austen. 49 William Degacher. 50 Thomas Llewelyn George Griffith. (RRWM)

The next morning after 'Black Wednesday', following the departure of the victorious Zulu Army and of Chelmsford's demoralised and weary force from the devastated battlefield area, only one living creature appeared to flourish. For days afterwards, in the dramatic words of Smith-Dorrien:

> ...the sky was darkened at times by continuous streams of 'aasvogels' [vultures], heading from all directions to the battlefield marked by that precipitous and conspicuous crag... Isandlhwana [sic] where nearly 900 British and 2,000 or 3,000 natives, friend and foe, had breathed their last on the fateful 22nd.
>
> Smith-Dorrien, *Forty-Eight Years'*, p.21

AFTER THE BATTLE

On 4 February, almost two weeks after the disaster, Major Wilsone-Black led a small tentative patrol from Rorke's Drift garrison, still recovering from their earlier stunning victory over the Zulu reserve, which discovered the assegaied, but still well-preserved, bodies of Lieutenants Melvill and Coghill. Lieutenant Harford himself recovered the Queen's Colour case and next day, nearby, in a quiet pool, the tattered remains of the silk Colour itself. Harford vividly recalled the earlier scene when the decaying bodies of Melvill and Coghill were found:

> Both were clearly recognisable. Melvill was in red, and Coghill in blue uniform. Both were lying on their backs about a yard from each other, Melvill at right angles to the path and Coghill parallel to it, a little above Melvill and with his head uphill. Both had been assegaied, but otherwise their bodies had been left untouched. Major Black at once said 'Now we shall see whether they have the Colours on them', and proceeded to unbutton Melvill's serge while I opened Coghill's patrol jacket but there were no Colours. Presently Major Black said, 'I wonder if Melvill's watch is on him, he always carried it in the small waist pocket of his breeches!', and on looking there was his gold watch which was subsequently sent to his widow. Nothing was found on Coghill, but his bad knee was still

51. Fugitive's Drift 1989: the cross marks the spot where Melvill and Coghill were found. (EY)

52. The Queen's Colour (on the left) is the colour rescued from the Buffalo River after Isandlwana. (RRWM)

> bandaged up. Undoubtedly, Melvill must have stuck to him and helped him along, otherwise he never could have got so far over such terrible ground.
>
> Harford, *The Zulu War Journal*, pp.49–50

A second, larger, patrol visited the battlefield of Isandlwana itself on 14 March, witnessed 'a horrid scene of desolation' as the 'still tainted air' filled their nostrils. Most of the Zulu dead had long been removed by their victorious compatriots, but over 100 wagons were left intact, the bodies of the 24th lying in:

> All conditions of horrible decay. Some were perfect skeletons, others that had not been stripped, or only partially so, were quite unapproachable and the stench was sickening; but with few exceptions it was impossible to recognise anyone and the only officer that was seen was discovered by his clothes. Of the regular soldiers the largest found in one place was sixty eight.
>
> Norris-Newman, *In Zululand*, p.123

A much larger force, including the 17th Lancers and commanded by Colonel Drury-Lowe, visited the wrecked Isandlwana campsite on 21 May 1879. By then, oats and mealies which had spilled from the food wagons had now sprouted around and through the liquefying corpses. Among the several journalists accompanying the force was Charles Norris-Newman of the *London Standard*. He discovered his own tent, or 'rather the disjecta membra of what had once been mine' and behind it, the 'dried-up bodies' of his servants and the skeletons of his horses. The site of Durnford's last stand on the Nek was also examined and the body of Durnford himself was identified in a patch of long grass, the distinctive long moustache still clinging to the withered skin of his face. He was easily recognisable:

> As he had on his Mess waistcoat, from the pocket of which Shepstone took a small pocket knife with his name on it; two rings were taken from the dead man's hand and presented with his knife… to his family.
>
> Norris-Newman, *In Zululand*, p.183

Perhaps the most distressing account of the massacre site was provided by Archibald Forbes, correspondent of the *Daily News*:

> The line of retreat towards Fugitive's Drift lay athwart a rocky slope to our right front with a precipitous ravine at its base. In

this ravine dead men lay thick – mere bones, with toughened, discoloured skin like leather covering them and clinging to them, the flesh all wasted away. Some were almost dismembered heaps of clammy yellow bones. I forbear to describe the faces with their blackened features and beards blanched by rain and sun. Each man had been disembowelled. Some were scalped and others subjected to yet ghastlier mutilation. The clothes had lasted better and helped to keep the skeletons together. All the way up the slope I traced, by the ghastly token of dead men, the fitful line of flight. Most of the men hereabouts were infantry of the 24th. It was like a long string with knots in it, the string formed of single corpses, the knots of clusters of dead where… little groups might have gathered to make a hopeless gallant stand and die. I came on a gully with a gun limber jammed in its edge, and the horses, their hides scarred with assegai stabs, hanging in their harnesses down the steep face of the ravine. A little further on was a broken and tattered ambulance wagon, with its team of mules, mouldering in their harness, and around lay the corpses of soldiers, poor helpless wretches, dragged out of an intercepted vehicle and done to death without chance of life.

On the crest or saddle, the slaughtered ones lay thick so that the string became a broad belt. Many hereabouts wore the uniform of the Natal Police… A strange dead calm reigned in this solitude of nature; grain had grown luxuriantly round the wagons, sprouting from the seed that dropped from the loads, falling in soil fertilised by the life-blood of gallant men… As one strolled aimlessly about one stumbled in the grass over skeletons that rattled to the touch. Here lay a corpse with a bayonet jammed into the mouth up to the socket, transfixing the head and mouth a foot into the ground. There lay a form that seemed cosily curled in a calm sleep, turned almost on its face, but seven assegai stabs have pierced the back. Most, however, lay flat on their backs with the arms stretched out and hands clenched. I noticed one dead man under a wagon with

> his head on a saddle for a pillow and a tarpaulin drawn over him, as if he had gone to sleep and died so… Close beside the dead, at the picquet line, a gully traverses the ground in front of the camp. About 400 paces beyond this was the ground of the battle before the troops broke from their formation and on both sides of the gully the dead lie thickly. In one place nearly fifty of the 24th lie almost touching as if they had fallen in rallying square. The line of straggling rush back to camp is clearly marked by skeletons all along the front.
>
> Moodie, *Moodie's Zulu War*, pp.251–52

Even hardened veterans were profoundly shocked by the scenes of devastation, in which even many camp pets had been killed by the rampant Zulu. A few escaped and survived, some arriving starved and exhausted at Rorke's Drift in the days following the disaster. They included Colonel Pulleine's pony and Lieutenant Daly's dog, 'Ponto'.

Tragically, it was to take nearly six months before the last of the garrison dead were buried. On 28 June 1879 the last scattered remains were interred, appropriately by 240 of their own regimental colleagues.

Battle Analysis: The Lessons of the Disaster

It is appropriate here to discuss the deeper reasons why the Isandlwana garrison had suffered such a catastrophic collapse. Virtually all the problems encountered by Pulleine's force can be traced back to the flaws in Chelmsford's initial battle plan.

Overextended Lines

First of all, the imperial lines were clearly overextended and highly susceptible to any flanking movement. Chelmsford's departing order to defend the camp had committed Pulleine to an impossible defence of what was, in effect, a great deal of unnecessary terrain. Vastly outnumbered, the only hope for

53. The rocky terrain and rough scrub which must have impeded the final British retreat to the tented area below the mountain. (EY)

Pulleine was to sustain a continuous imperial volley fire. This, in turn, depended on an uninterrupted supply of ammunition and it was here that Chelmsford's disposition of the campsite played a crucial role in precipitating the disaster. Virtually all sources agree that the excessive distance of Durnford's mounted colonial forces from the main ammunition supply was almost certainly the key factor in the collapse of the right wing. Jabez Molife, one of the few survivors from Durnford's command, vividly recalled that after the initial check to the Zulu left horn, 'our cartridges were nearly done', with inexplicable delays in securing fresh ammunition from the camp. As historian Ian Knight confirms, Durnford's collapse would have desperate consequences for Pulleine's line effectively out-flanking the infantry on the right and the rear.

It is possible that the British left wing was also severely compromised by its distance from the two ammunition wagons of the 1st and 2nd Battalion, 24th Regiment. Captain Henry Hallam Parr confirmed that Cavaye's, Mostyn's and Dyson's men, almost certainly fatigued after their rapid return from the Spur and being longest in the firing line, were:

A New Ammunition Supply Theory

A recent fascinating theory in relation to the ammunition controversy at Isandlwana has thrown fresh light on this still contentious area. Recently, distinguished military historian Colonel Ian Bennett (RLC retired), discovered that Martini-Henry rifle and carbine cartridges 'were not strictly compatible'. This suggested to him another reason why, at Isandlwana, 'Quartermasters of the 24th Foot refused to issue ammunition to men of the Natal Native Horse' who were 'armed with Swinburne-Henry carbines'. Regular army quartermasters, he points out, 'would have had the technical expertise to know that while the chambers of both weapons were of a similar bore, the cartridges were different'. In comparison with rifle rounds, 'those for carbines were an eighth of an inch shorter, the bullet weighed less and the powder charge was smaller'. Rifle cartridges fired from a carbine, he significantly observes, 'caused a greater recoil, were liable to jam, and fell eleven inches lower in trajectory'. Unfortunately at the time of the Zulu War both cartridges were of similar appearance, 'the bullets being wrapped with two twists of white paper'. He notes: 'in the aftermath of the Zulu War, new regulations were introduced to ensure that carbine cartridges could be readily distinguished from those of Martini-Henry rifles'. New distinguishing marks on the sides and ends of each ammunition box were also introduced, those for rifles 'carried a solid red rectangle', while those for carbines 'carried a red rectangle in outline only'.

While leading authorities such as Ian Knight and Lieutenant Snook strongly contend that British ammunitions supply and staffing problems at Isandlwana were either never an issue or were merely used to explain or excuse the stunning Zulu victory, it is clear from this and my own and other theories that the ammunition debate can never be irrevocably resolved either way. (Source: Colonel I. Bennett Correspondence, *Soldiers of the Queen: Journal of the Victorian Military Society*, Issue 113, June 2003, p.1)

> ...very short of ammunition and their initial accoutrement of only seventy round apiece was rapidly expended owing to the hot fire that they had been forced to sustain to keep the Zulus from closing upon them while they were retreating on the camp.
>
> Hallam Parr, *Sketch*, pp.211–12

Firing an average of three rounds per minute, one source estimates that the imperial infantry alone expended up to 70,000 rounds during the first half hour of the main battle.

Ammunition Shortages

Ammunition distribution was clearly not helped by the inflexible nature of quartermastering. At least one quartermaster, Edward Bloomfield of the 2/24th Foot, was recorded as obdurately refusing the issue of cartridges to 'non battalion' members, culminating in a confrontation between Lieutenant Smith-Dorrien, who was still desperately trying to feed the imperial firing lines. As the latter rifled through his battalion's ammunition boxes, he apparently remonstrated; 'For heavens sake don't take that man for it belongs to our battalion'. To which Smith-Dorrien replied, 'Hang it all man, you don't want a requisition now, do you?' Similar scenes elsewhere behind the British lines give equal credence to ammunition supply problems. NNC Commander, Captain Barton, provided telling evidence. He told *London Standard* correspondent

54. Edward Bloomfield 2/24th, one of two quartermasters who controlled the logistical lifelines at Isandlwana. (RRWM)

55. Quartermaster James Pullen 1/24th. (RRWM)

Norris-Newman that his mounted 'Amangwane' men:

> ...really fought well at their first charge and until all the ammunition was exhausted; they were then compelled to fall back on the camp, where they sought for a fresh supply of ammunition. Unfortunately, this was refused by the officer in charge as it would all be required by the infantry themselves. This was assuredly a fatal error of judgement.
>
> Norris-Newman, *In Zululand*, p.63

The early recorded death of Quartermaster Bloomfield, possibly due to Zulu gunfire, must have also greatly exacerbated the ammunition supply situation. Similarly the otherwise brave action of the other key 1/24th quartermaster, James Pullen, may have massively added to the supply difficulties. He abandoned his post to lead reinforcements for the beleagured British right wing. Survivor James Brickhill witnessed his premature departure from this critical post:

> Above the 1/24 camp I met my poor tent companion, Quartermaster Pullen, who shouted to the running soldiers, 'come on men rally here, follow me. Don't be running away like a parcel of women. Let's try and turn their flank.' Turning to me he said, 'Mr Brickhill, do go to Colonel Pulleine and ask him to send us help, as they are out-flanking us here on the right.' He went away towards the front of the stoney kopje followed by several of the soldiers.
>
> Hattersley, *Annals*, p.154

A Famous Isandlwana Survivor

One of the few European survivors of Isandlwana went on to become one of the most prominent generals of the First World War.

Lieutenant Horace Lockwood Smith-Dorrien, 95th Regiment (1858–1930), after playing a heroic role in supporting and rallying the British left wing at Isandlwana and then attempting to maintain the ammunition supply line in the central camp area, narrowly escaped death after a horrendous pursuit by several Zulu warriors. Crossing brutal terrain after the lines collapsed and in an exhausted state he found refuge at the British outpost Helpmekaar.

Following this nightmare experience his military fortunes steadily improved and in 1882 he was engaged in the suppression of the 1882 Egyptian nationalist revolt and later in the 1885 Anglo-Sudanese War. He also participated in the Tirah Campaign on the Northwest Frontier and in the 1899–1902 Boer War. After serving in India as Adjutant General and Commander of the Fourth Division he returned to Britain in 1907 to command the Aldershot Garrison.

On the outbreak of the First World War he was given command of the British II Corps in France under overall command of Sir John French. After the retreat from Mons, Smith-Dorrien took the courageous, if controversial, decision, against his commander's orders, to hold the line in order to facilitate a more organised withdrawal. French accused him of disobeying orders for what was a costly action but one which was later considered by many to be tactically justified. He was removed from command of II Corps and later, after further criticism, resigned his command altogether. He returned to Britain in May 1915. Smith-Dorrien retired from the army in 1922 and he was later tragically killed in a car crash near Chippenham, Wiltshire in 1930.

(Source: H. Smith-Dorrien, *Isandlwana to the Great War*, reprint, Leonaur Books 2009)

Private Bickley, 1/24th, provides further crucial supporting evidence of Pullen's premature abandonment of his post on the 1/24th ammunition wagon, just as the regulars were retreating back to the camp area:

> The Quartermaster then came up and asked me if I could saddle his horse for him… he left the horse tied up by the Head Stall, but I saw no more of the Quartermaster who had gone away in the direction of the officers' latrine. By this time all the idlers were clearing out of the camp and the skirmishers driven in…
>
> Holme, *Silver Wreath*, p.46

The alleged panic of elements of the NNC, who may, it has been suggested, have caused a break on the British left flank, remains hotly contested today. But widespread panic on their part would have been quite understandable as they were poorly equipped, averaging only ten rifles per company. Indeed a collapse there would have more seriously damaged the central defensive position than Durnford's known collapse or retreat on the far right. Private Grant, 1/24th, having earlier escaped the destruction of the Rocket Battery, found, on his return to camp, that it was the, 'Companies on the left' which were 'completely surrounded by the enemy and everyone was making the best of their way out of the camp'. This would tally with the evidence of Private Williams, 1/24th, who recalled the effective severance of this logistical lifeline by the panicking NNC contingents who were rapidly joined by scores of camp casuals:

> The men in Camp, Bandsmen and men on guard etc were trying to take ammunition to the companies but the greater part never got there as I saw horses and mules with ammunition on their backs galloping about the camp a short time afterwards.
>
> Holme, *Silver Wreath*, pp.47–48, Williams Account

Clearly, many of the camp stragglers rounded up by Lieutenants Essex and Smith-Dorrien earlier in the battle to help supply the imperial firing lines were now either fleeing their posts, or had been swept along by the mass exodus through the camp. Private E. Wilson, a 1/24th stretcher bearer, recalled the knock-on effect of this panic-stricken flight upon even those hard-pressed military units still supporting the front lines:

> …when the idlers and men among the tents were making the best of their way out of the camp the doctor told us that we were no longer likely to be of any use and the band sergeant told us we had better get away as best we could.
>
> Holme, *Silver Wreath*, p.48

It was perhaps this deadly human and logistical chaos reigning within the camp that inspired Pulleine to recall the remaining intact imperial companies in a last desperate attempt to bypass the collapsing supply lines and conduct an organised defence based solidly upon the ammunition wagons. Private Bickley, a 1/24th survivor, probably witnessed this critical moment just before the bugler called the retreat:

> The companies out skirmishing were now apparently getting short of ammunition… and the Native Contingent had been driven into the camp and, together, with most of the transport other employed natives were rushing out of the camp towards the road to Rorke's Drift.
>
> Holme, *Silver Wreath*, p.46

Moreover, even where the runners were reaching the rifle companies, demand may well have been exceeding supply. With the leading Zulu formation '100 to 150 yards distant' from the frontlines, the rate of fire and ammunition expenditure must have increased immensely. As Private Williams recalled, 'when

56. Lieutenant Horace Smith-Dorrien as a brigadier general. (JY)

the natives fell back on the camp we fired 40 to 50 rounds each'. What could only have been a few minutes later – as Zulus appeared not only from the left and right but ultimately from the last escape route at the rear of the Nek – he 'got 40 rounds more ammunition' of which he 'then used 29'. Indeed, it is only a natural human tendency to massively increase your rate of firing when your enemy is within yards of killing you! Lieutenant Mainwaring's sketch map of Isandlwana, prepared on behalf of the Intelligence Branch months after the battle, confirmed the 'signs of heavy fighting' along the 'southern crest line' occupied by Pope's, Wardell's and Porteous's centre companies, an area 'strewn with empty cartridge cases'.

Moreover, we know that large numbers of men of these three centre line companies had survived the final retreat into the tented areas. Major Wilsone-Black's subsequent reports on the battlefield confirmed the paucity of bodies in the firing line, and the heaviest concentration of 24th corpses around the 1/24th tented areas and wagons on the Nek. Indeed, Lieutenant Higginson of the NNC recalled the number of men coming in from the outlying companies searching for ammunition, and that although the men of the second battalion (NNC) were 'running', the 24th were 'retreating also but very slowly'. At least two companies were seen still intact, kneeling and firing even in the camp area.

57. Francis Pender Porteous, imperial officer of the 24th Regiment. (RRWM)

In the event, effectively deprived of their ammunition supply, these imperial regulars were left to fight for their lives either individually, or in small groups, with possibly one weakly formed square established behind the 1/24th tented area. They were clearly doomed and most probably died in a matter of minutes. As one Zulu eyewitness recalled, with direct reference to a failing ammunition supply:

> Your people, when, as in several instances, only numbering three, would stand back to back and defy us to approach. While the ammunition lasted, we did not attack; but took advantage of them when their powder failed. We allowed none to escape.
>
> Hattersley, *Annals*, p.261

Among the last stands in and above the camp area, notably Durnford's mixed group of regulars and colonials on the Nek, and Younghusband's sixty-odd men trapped on a ledge of the Isandlwana Crag, there is evidence, however, of last-ditch attempts to rectify what had become a deadly logistical nightmare. One Zulu eyewitness, Uguku, significantly noticed how 'one party of soldiers came out from among the tents and formed up a little above the ammunition wagons'. The last desperate charge of another group 'on the steep slope under the cliff behind the camp' (Younghusband's survivors) may well have been aimed at reaching one of the precious ammunition wagons. A Zulu of the uNokhenke recalled that:

> They fought well… and the Zulus could not get at them at all; they were shot and bayoneted as fast as they came up. At last the soldiers gave a shout and charged down upon us… they killed themselves by running down, for our people got above them and quite surrounded them; these and a group of white men on the Nek were the last to fall.
>
> Emery, *Red Soldier*, p.84

The fate of 'a group of white men on the Nek' (along with Lieutenant Anstey's final stand a couple of miles along Fugitive's Drift, probably the last to die), was witnessed by a fleeing 'government conductor of wagons'. He provided a fleeting glimpse of a last attempt by elements of Durnford's group to restore the broken ammunition supply line:

> When I left the camp Colonel Durnford was still alive as well as a small remnant of the Regulars, but they were so hemmed

58. An unusual view of the rear of Isandlwana from Fugitive's Drift, where the Undi Corps began its advance on Rorke's Drift. (EY)

> in that escape was impossible, and their ammunition seemed expended, for artillery men were trying to break open the cases on the wagons to supply them but it was too late.
>
> Norris-Newman, *In Zululand*, pp.78–79

The Zulu eyewitness Mehlokazulu, attached to the iNgobamakhosi Regiment, provided a fitting epitaph to the possible role of ammunition failure in this imperial disaster. Examining the corpses, mainly of the 1st and 2nd, 24th Regiment after the battle in the camp area, he tellingly observed:

> We searched the pouches of the men; some had a few cartridges, most of them had none at all; there were very few found. Some had cartouche boxes, other cartridge belts: the belts were all empty, but a few cartridges were found in a few of the cartouche boxes.
>
> Norris-Newman, *In Zululand*, p.83

Absence of Defensive Fortifications

While the ammunition supply controversy may never be finally resolved, Chelmsford's (and to a lesser extent Pulleine's and Durnford's) failure to establish a final reserve or bastion of defence certainly played a major role in the disaster. The absence of any laagering of the wagons, and of entrenchments, meant that the troops, once in retreat, stood no chance of recovering or stabilising their position. Had there been a final redoubt position (as later at Rorke's Drift), possibly in square formations at the base of the Isandlwana Mountain, or grouped around the vital ammunition wagons, many more men might have survived. Years later, Lieutenant Stafford observed that:

> I can never understand to this day why this was not done. The advice to form laager in every camp when campaigning against Zulus, had been told and retold to the British by their Boer advisers over and over again. It was the old, old mistake of underrating

> an enemy that has been made by the British before and since the fatal mistake at Isandhlwana... Had a laager been formed at Isandhlwana with the wagons, boulders, boxes etc we could have withstood the Zulu armies at any rate until such time as reinforcements arrived.
>
> NAM, Stafford Papers

In the event, devoid of such physical protection and vastly outnumbered, men were left to perish alone or in small vulnerable groups.

Underestimation of the Zulu Enemy

Thirdly, Chelmsford, Durnford, and again to a much lesser extent Pulleine, had clearly totally misjudged not only the mobility but the sheer raw courage, fighting spirit and resilience of the Zulu Army. Even at the height of the battle – the uKhandempemvu, uMbonambi and iNgobamakhosi regiments in particular were decimated at as little as 150 yards' range – there had been no Zulu mass panic and no attempt to retreat. When the imperial lines, arguably starved of ammunition, were fatally outflanked and had finally wavered, the Zulu bravery and overall fighting spirit was graphically symbolised by the rallying calls of several brave *indunas*, notably Mkhosana and Ndlaka of the uKhandempemvu. The latter, before being killed by a rifle bullet to the head, fully exposed himself to the British firing line in order to rally his warriors for the final ferocious charge. Zulu sustained resistance and resilience to the hitherto unchallenged destructive power of the Martini-Henry rifle was, undoubtedly, a major contributory factor to the eventual defeat of Pulleine's force. It was, in essence, a stunning Zulu victory.

Division of Forces

Finally, Chelmsford's fatal decision to divide his force early that morning undoubtedly represented a major tactical error. By 1pm at the critical moment of the battle, Chelmsford's force was at least 3 hours' marching time away and any possibility of rescue and reinforcement was out of the question. In the interim period, after the first message from Pulleine (received at 9.30am), Chelmsford had stubbornly sustained his aloof attitude to the steady procession of reports and rumours of fighting occurring within his camp area.

In mitigation, neither Chelmsford nor his subordinate commanders, in their long military experience, had ever before confronted such a formidable enemy as the Zulu. Nevertheless, the poor initial defence plans and the misjudged decision to divert to the south-east were both negligent acts bordering on recklessness. To the end of his days, even after the subsequent Court of Inquiry, Chelmsford never admitted to his direct culpability for this disastrous failure of his battle plans. Much of the blame, as we shall see, was shifted firstly onto the unfortunate Glyn, then, more conveniently, onto the shoulders of the deceased Durnford, and, to a much lesser extent, Pulleine, for overextending their lines. In Chelmsford's obdurate view, 'the rear was perfectly secure… I consider never was there a position where a small force could have made a better defensive stand'. But in other correspondence, addressed to both Sir Bartle Frere and to his column commanders, Chelmsford admitted to his underestimation of the 'heavier numbers of Zulu' attacking his depleted force and, above all, the 'desperate bravery of the Zulu which had been the subject of much astonishment'. This is not to say that Durnford was blameless. His hasty gung-ho decision to conduct a morning foray against a hitherto unknown enemy on the Nqutu Heights arguably overextended an already weakened camp garrison and put unnecessary pressure on the combat inexperienced Lieutenant Colonel Pulleine.

THE LEGACY

The news of the military catastrophe at Isandlwana on 11 February 1879 had come, as we have seen, as a terrible shock to both the government and people of Britain. As Hicks Beach's somewhat ambivalent despatches immediately before the war had indicated, both Sir Bartle Frere and Lord Chelmsford were likely to pay a heavy political price if the war was not conducted cheaply and with minimum casualties. By mid-February 1879, as the full extent of the tragedy became clear, the '*isangoma*' ('witchfinders') of press and parliament had commenced a vitriolic campaign demanding for the recall of both men. It soon became clear that Disraeli's government needed scapegoats. As one Colonial Office official, Edward Fairfield, cryptically observed in a Minute on 10 March, 'the war and, above all, the defeat of Isandula have totally changed the case'. *The Times* on 12 February was much more explicit: 'There is, in fact, little room for doubt that if Lord Chelmsford's invasion had been successful, Sir Bartle Frere's conduct would have been condoned.

Given this major military disaster 'somebody must be fixed for the blame' as one speaker in the House of Commons so aptly put it. The Prime Minister, the earl of Beaconsfield, Benjamin Disraeli, was particularly stunned by the disaster and now forced to despatch urgent and costly reinforcements to Natal, was privately furious with both Frere and Chelmsford. The disaster at Isandlwana would, he asserted, 'change everything, reduce our continental influence and embarrass our resources'. Moreover, even after the subsequent Court of Inquiry, held in late January 1879, Chelmsford continued to deny his direct culpability for this disastrous failure of his battle plans. In a memorandum dated 20 February 1879, there was even an attempt by Chelmsford to assign much of the blame for the disaster to his No. 3 Column Commander, Colonel Richard Glyn. He wrote:

> I have no desire whatever to shift any of the responsibility which probably belongs to me on to the shoulders of the officers commanding No. 3 Column. At the same time I am anxious to make it clear that, by accompanying No. 3 Column, I did not accept the responsibility for the numerous details which necessarily have to be considered by an officer commanding a Column in the field. On arriving at the camp of No. 3 Column I myself emphasised personally to Colonel Glyn that I did not wish to interfere in anyway with the Commander of the Column but that, of course, I should be only to glad to talk over with him all matters connected with it, and to give him the benefit of my opinion whenever he required it – I believe that I also said the same of Major Clery my Senior Staff Officer.

While admitting:

> As regards the movement of the Column and the several reconnaissances made by portions of that column, I was entirely responsible… my orders, however, were always conveyed to Colonel Glyn in plenty of time for him to consider and to reflect upon things; and I consider that I have a right to assume that if Colonel Glyn considers that any such orders were any way likely to be injurious to the interest of any portion of his force, or that my proposed movements were in any way hazardous, he would have at once have brought the fact to my notice.

He continued further to say that, 'I consider Colonel Glyn was bound to inform me if at any time his own judgement differed from mine regarding the movement I was anxious to carry out'.

Chelmsford concluded:

> No such objection was ever made and I assume therefore that orders by me received his approval. As regards outposts, patrolling and the ordinary precautions for the safety of the camp, I, on arriving at the camp of No. 3 Column, considered that for all these arrangements Colonel Glyn was solely responsible and had I interfered in such matters it would have been tantamount to my taking direct command of the Column, a position in which I deprecated from the first.
>
> Chelmsford Memorandum, 20 February 1879

It was a position which directly contradicted Clery's earlier private letter that claimed that Lord Chelmsford had effectively assumed command of the force and had become involved in very minute operational detail. The extent of the cover-up for the Isandlwana disaster is beyond the scope of this relatively short battle study but the 27 January inquiry held at Helpmekaar, based largely on the evidence of the five surviving imperial officers, conveniently blamed desertion and panic by Britain's African allies as the primary cause.

Whoever was responsible at ground level, with Pulleine and Durnford both dead it was Frere and Chelmsford who were initially destined to bear the brunt of the blame. Over the weeks following the disaster, both men were subjected to brutal criticism, locally in the Cape and at home in the Houses of Parliament. During the South African debates in the House of Lords on 26 March 1879, Lord Lansdowne 'complained generally of Sir Bartle Frere's conduct and pointed out that if the Government was not satisfied with Sir Bartle Frere's conduct they were bound to recall him. This motion was treated as a motion of censure' Similarly, Lord Cranbrook made a most effective speech, admitting that Sir Bartle Frere ought to have consulted the government before sending the ultimatum to the Zulu king and stated that Sir Michael Hicks Beach had notified this in very plain terms to Sir Bartle Frere.

In the later Commons 'South African debate', a leading MP, Sir Robert Peel, 'made a really virulent attack on Sir Bartle Frere' and then 'took it into his head to make a still more virulent attack on Lord Chelmsford whom he denounced as being worthy of Admiral Byng'.

These political criticisms were paralleled by fierce attacks launched against Frere and Chelmsford from within the Victorian military establishment. Before the results of the Court of Inquiry had been received, the Adjutant General, on behalf of the Duke of Cambridge, the Commander-in-Chief of the British Army, had already sent to Chelmsford a highly critical memorandum for which answers were immediately required. In addition to criticisms of Chelmsford's deployment of the camp, including the lack of laagering and entrenchment and the splitting of his forces, Chelmsford was even lambasted for his earlier deployment of the Rorke's Drift supply depot, notwithstanding the victory already achieved there. He was asked: 'how did it happen that the post at Rorke's Drift, covering as it did the passage into Zululand, was not put into a state of defence previous to your Lordships advance to Isandula hill'. General Sir Garnet Wolseley and the officers from his school 'were even more scathing in their public and private criticism of both Frere and Chelmsford, but particularly Chelmsford. Wolseley wrote to his wife asserting that Chelmsford, 'has violated every principle of war in his plan of campaign, and has, in fact, courted disaster'. In his private diary he was even more brutal in his assessment of Chelmsford's tactics at Isandlwana and particularly the performance of some of his officers. He wrote:

> Heroes have been made of men like Melvill and Coghill who, taking advantage of their having horses, bolted from the scene of action to save their lives. If the 24th had been well handled and had behaved well then the disaster could never have occurred, much as Chelmsford, by his ignorance of Zulu tactics, had left them exposed to attack.
>
> Preston, *Wolseley's South African Journal, 1879–80*, pp.256–57

59. Lieutenant General Sir Garnet Wolseley, who superceded Chelmsford as commander-in-chief, but became embittered when Chelmsford thwarted his opportunity for glory by finally breaking Zulu power at Ulundi. (JY)

60. A satirical comment on Wolseley's final capture of the elusive Cetshwayo long after the British victory at Ulundi, from Punch*, September 1879. (EY)*

Leading white settlers in the local area added to the tide of criticism of Chelmsford's tactics and, some like Wolseley, but even more controversially, indicated that widespread panic and desertion by *both* European troops and their African allies had been a factor in the defeat. The Mayor of Durban, George Cato, wrote to his son-in-law:

> Every word of caution I gave to anybody that would listen to me has been verified. Nothing new in all the Zulu tactics, The Head Camp was no Camp. All wagons, tents etc scattered everywhere and the Zulus came on like waves on the ocean shore: never stopped, never shouted or said a word until our fellows, black and white bolted. They then gave a shout and rushed at the Camp and in five minutes there was not a man left. The Zulus poured in a shower of assegais and rushed to the charge, very few Zulus were killed in the camp; but they were mowed down as they advanced and the Rifles got so hot that men could hardly hold them. Some that could dipped them in water. There is no question that the troops were out-generalled.
>
> G.C. Cato to Richards, 2 Feb.1879, Banks collection

Others, including Essex, also revealed at the inquiry, that, at the climax of the battle, 'the men became unsteady' (a possible reference to temporary battlefield jitters by the younger, less experienced soldiers of the 2/24th) and at least one Zulu informant thought the British 'fought like cowards; they shot at us when we were far away but they wanted to run away when we arrived'. However, as the mass of evidence in this and other leading works already indicate, and as Lieutenant Colonel Snook so recently reasserted in his book *How Men Can Die Better*, the vast majority of the regular infantrymen and their officers, like their gallant Zulu opponents, fought extremely well and to the death.

Rorke's Drift

If Isandlwana was the defeat that the Empire tried to hide away and forget, Rorke's Drift was the victory that they couldn't help but celebrate. Perhaps the awarding of eleven Victoria Crosses for the engagement was testament to the jubilation at such a swift turnaround in the situation. Around 140 British and colonial troops defended the garrison against the onslaught of over 4,000 Zulus, with the fighting culminating on 23 January, just one day after the ignominy of Isandlwana. Over 400 Zulus were killed for the loss of only seventeen British dead. Certainly, the victory made the Isandlwana defeat easier to swallow and easier to sweep under the carpet, but equally this should not take away from the extreme heroism demonstrated on both sides.

Postscript

As an almost unique example of a stunning victory by an indigenous people over its far better-armed colonial adversaries, the battle of Isandlwana has rightly retained its iconic status in Zulu folklore and historical memory. This is despite the almost unbroken succession of heavy defeats subsequently inflicted upon them by the British at Rorke's Drift, Inyenzane, Gingindlovu and Khambula, culminating most tragically at oNdini or Ulundi in July 1879, where the old Zulu order was finally broken. But such defeats were perhaps inevitable at the hands of a now more prepared and technically superior enemy and do not detract at all from the significance of this great Zulu victory. Isandlwana still fully justifies itself as a proud and integral part of modern Zulu heritage and national identity.

For the British, their memory of the battle, although the subject of much contemporary consternation, was eventually overshadowed by the far larger scale and casualty levels of the First and Second World Wars. This was despite the great fiftieth commemoration of January 1929, staged on the battlefield itself, which was attended

61. In this Punch *cartoon Lieutenants Chard and Bromhead are saluted for their gallant defence at Rorke's Drift, March 1879.*

by scores of Zulu and European veterans and which was widely reported in local South African newspapers. During the immediate post-Second World War period, however, with the publication of two major books by Professor Reginald Coupland and Donald Morris, and the distribution of two major films on the Zulu War, Isandlwana has become a subject of renewed popular fascination. The 1964 film *Zulu*, although based largely on the battle of Rorke's Drift, featured stunning opening scenes of the Isandlwana massacre, while a 1979 follow-up *Zulu Dawn*, powerfully depicted (notwithstanding serious budget and script problems), a graphic portrayal of the build-up and climax of this legendary battle. Following these extremely popular, if by no means historically accurate films, the post-100th anniversary of the battle has witnessed a plethora of literature and TV documentaries focused specifically on Isandlwana. Meanwhile, this still evocative battlefield has continued to attract vast numbers of visitors from across the world, ensuring that its memory will endure for many more years to come.

ORDERS OF BATTLE

British Army

No. 2 Column (Colonel Durnford, Royal Engineers)

11/7th Brigade, Royal Artilley
Natal Native Horse

1/1st Natal Native Contingent
2/1st Natal Native Contingent

No. 3 Column (Lieutenant Colonel Pulleine)

N/5th Brigade, Royal Horse Artillery
5th Field Company, Royal Engineers
1/24th Regiment of Foot
2/24th Regiment of Foot
90th Regiment of Foot
Army Service Corps
Army Hospital Corps
Imperial Mounted Infantry
Natal Mounted Police
Natal Carbineers
Newcastle Mounted Rifles
Buffalo Border Guard
Natal Native Pioneer Corps
1/3rd Natal Native Contingent
2/3rd Natal Native Contingent

Zulu Force (approx positionings)

Right horn

uDududu Regiment
uNokhenke Regiment
iMbube Regiment
iSangqu Regiment

Chest

uKhandampemvu Regiment
uMbonambi Regiment

Left horn

iNgobamakhosi Regiment
uMbonambi Regiment
uVe Regiment

Reserve

Undi Corps comprising:
- uDloko Regiment
- uThulwana Regiment
- inDlondlo Regiment

FURTHER READING

Recommended archives: National Archives (formerly Public Record Office), Kew (papers referenced throughout this book and held in their collections include: Colonial (CO) and War Office (WO) files; National Army Museum (NAM); Royal Regiment of Wales Museum (RRWM); *Illustrated London News* (*ILN*); and Killie Campbell Library, South Africa.

Primary Sources

Papers referenced and quoted from in text:
CO 48/482, Carnarvon to Frere, 23 Dec. 1878
CO 48/486, Chelmsford to Secretary of State for War, 27 Oct. 1878
CO 48/486, Tel. Hicks Beach to Frere, 5 Oct. 1878
CO 48/486, Wingfield Note, 16 Sept. 1878
CO 48/487, Frere Memo, 13 Nov. 1878
CO 79/126, Fairfield to Bramston Minute, 10 Mar. 1879
CO, Herbert Note, 13 Dec. 1878
ILN, Isandlwana Court of Inquiry, Capt. Nourse evidence, 17 Mar. 1879
ILN, Isandlwana Court of Inquiry, Cochrane evidence, 17 Mar. 1879
ILN, Isandlwana Court of Inquiry, Essex evidence, 17 Mar. 1879
India Office Library, Political and Secret Memoranda, File A2, Frere Minute, 6 Dec. 1863
Martineau, 2, p.230, Bulwer to Carnarvon, 2 Nov. 1876
Martineau, p.272, Chelmsford Memo, 8 Jan. 1879
NAM, Chelmsford Papers, Adjutant General to Chelmsford, 6 Mar. 1879
NAM, Chelmsford Papers, Raw Account
RA Queen Victoria's Journal, Disraeli to HM, 12 Feb. 1879
RA VIC/034/29, South Africa, Duke of Richmond to HM, 26 Mar. 1879
RA VIC/034/29, South Africa, Sir Stafford Northcote to HM, 1 Apr. 1879
RRWM, Clery Memo, 18 Feb. 1879
RRWM, Kilvert Diary, 11 Feb. 1879

St Aldwyn/Hicks Beach Papers, Hicks Beach to Frere, 7 Mar. and 4 Apr. 1878
St Aldwyn/Hicks Beach Papers, Hicks Beach to Frere, 10 Oct. 1878
St Aldwyn/Hicks Beach Papers, Hicks Beach to Disraeli, 17 Oct. and 3 Nov. 1878
St Aldwyn/Hicks Beach Papers, Hicks Beach to Frere, 11 Dec. 1878
St Aldwyn/Hicks Beach Papers, Frere to Hicks Beach, 25 Apr. 1879
The Times, 12 Feb. 1879
The Times, Essex letter, 2 Apr. 1879

Select Bibliography

Please note page numbers denote where quotes in the text have been referenced from.

Arthur, Sir G., *The Letters of Lord and Lady Wolseley* (William Heinemann, 1922)
Atkinson, C.T., *The South Wales Borderers, 24th Foot* (Cambridge University Press, 1937) pp.332–33
Barnett, C., *Britain and her Army* (Weidenfeld & Nicholson, 2000)
Beckett, I., *Isandlwana 1879* (Brasseys, 2003)
Bennett, I.H.W., *Eyewitness in Zululand* (Greenhill Books, 1989)
Castle, I., British Infantryman in South Africa (Osprey, 2003)
Clements, W.H., *The Glamour and Tragedy of the Zulu War* (Lane, 1936) pp.59, 63
Coupland, Sir R., *Zulu Battle Piece: Isandhlwana* (Collins, 1948)
David, S., *Zulu: The Heroism and Tragedy of the Zulu War of 1879* (Penguin Books, 2004) pp.28–29, 42
De Kiewiet, C.W., *The Imperial Factor in South Africa* (Frank Cass Publishers, 1965) p.127
Duminy A. and C. Ballard (eds), *The Anglo-Zulu War: New Perspectives* (University of Natal Press, 1981)
Emery, F., *Red Soldier: Letters from the Zulu War*, 1879 (Hodder and Stoughton, 1977)
Gardiner, A.G., *Life of Sir William Harcourt*, vol. 2 (Constable, 1923), p.349.
Goodfellow, C.F., *Great Britain and South African Confederation* (Oxford University Press, 1966) pp.18–22 (for an excellent discussion of military literacy levels)
Greaves, A., *Isandlwana* (Cassell, 2001)
Greaves, A. and I. Knight, *Who's Who in the Zulu War 1879*, 2 vols (Pen and Sword, 2006)
Guy, J., *The Destruction of the Zulu Kingdom* (Longman, 1979)
Hallam Parr, Capt. H.A., *Sketch of the Zulu and Kafir Wars* (C. Kegan Paul, 1880) pp.180, 183, 185, 188
Harford, H., D. Child (ed.) *The Zulu War Journal of Colonel Henry Harford* (Shuter and Shooter, 1978) p.19, 24
Hattersley, A.F., *Later Annals of Natal* (Longmans, Green and Co., 1938) p.153
Hicks Beach, Lady V., *Life of Sir Michael Hicks Beach* (Macmillan & Co., 1932)
Holme, N., *Silver Wreath: Being the 24th Regiment at Isandlwana and Rorke's*

Drift 1879 (Samson Books, 1979) pp.46 (Bickley Account), 47, 48 (Williams Account)

Jackson, F.W.D., *Hill of the Sphinx* (Westerners Publications, 2003)

Knight, I., *Zulu Rising: The Epic Story of Isandlwana and Rorke's Drift* (Macmillan, 2010) pp.360, 377–81 (for discussion of ammunition situation), 389, 420

Knight, I., *The Battles of Isandlwana and Rorke's Drift* (Windrow and Greene, 1992) pp.62, 84

Laband, J., *Lord Chelmsford's Zululand Campaign, 1878–79* (Army Records Society, 1994) pp.78, 92–93

Laband, J., *Rope of Sand, The Rise and Fall of the Zulu Kingdom in the Nineteenth Century* (Jonathan Ball, 1995)

Lock, R., and P. Quantrill, *Zulu Victory: The epic of Isandlwana and the cover-up* (Greenhill Books, 2002) pp.322–27 (for discussion of ammunition situation)

Lock, R., and P. Quantrill (eds) *The Red Book: Natal Press Reports Anglo-Zulu War 1879* (Anglo-Zulu War Historical Society, 1990) p.22

Mitford, B., *Through the Zulu Country: Its Battlefields and its People* (Kegan, Paul, Trench and Co., 1883)

Moodie, D.C.F., *Moodie's Zulu War* (N&S Press, 1988) pp.25–6, 43–4

Morley, R.J., *Life of Gladstone*, vol. 2 (Macmillan, 1903), p.592

Morris, D.R., *The Washing of the Spears* (Jonathan Cape, 1966) pp.367, 375

Norris-Newman, C.L., *In Zululand with the British throughout the war of 1879*, (W.H. Allen, 1880)

Rothwell, J.S. (compiler), 'Narrative of Field Operations connected with the Zulu War of 1879' (War Office, London, 1881, reprinted 1907 and 1989)

Smith-Dorrien, H., *Memories of Forty-Eight Years' Service* (J. Murray, 1925) pp.14, 16–17

Snook, Lieutenant Colonel M., *How Can Men Die Better: The Secrets of Isandlwana Revealed* (Greenhill Books, 2005) pp.11–12

Spiers, E., *The Late Victorian Army* (Manchester University Press, 1992) (See for detailed studies of the development of the Victorian British Army)

Worsfold, B., *Sir Bartle Frere: A Footnote to the History of the British Empire* (Thornton Butterworth Ltd, 1923) p.24

Yorke, E.J., *Zulu* (Tempus/The History Press, 2005)

Yorke, E.J., *Playing the Great Game, Britain, War and Politics in Afghanistan 1839–2009* (Robert Hayes Books, 2011) (See chapters 5 and 6 for a discussion on troubles elsewhere during the period)

Yorke, E.J., 'Underestimating the Enemy: Isandlwana 1879' in *The Hutchinson Atlas of Battle Plans: Before and After* (Helicon Books, 1998) pp.165–78

Yorke, E.J., 'Isandlwana, 1879, Further Reflections on the Ammunition Controversy', *Journal of the Society of Army Historical Research*, 1994

Young, J., *They Fell like Stones: Battles and Casualties of the Zulu War*, (Greenhill Books, 1991) pp.22–3 (for details of the British ultimatum)

INDEX